REALMS OF THE
LIVING DEAD

Teachings of
The Order of Christian Mystics

REALMS OF THE
LIVING DEAD

TEACHINGS OF THE ORDER OF CHRISTIAN MYSTICS

THE "CURTISS BOOKS" FREELY AVAILABLE AT

WWW.ORDEROFCHRISTIANMYSTICS.CO.ZA

REALMS OF THE LIVING DEAD

A BRIEF DESCRIPTION OF LIFE AFTER DEATH

Transcribed by
HARRIETTE AUGUSTA CURTISS
and
F. HOMER CURTISS, B.S., M.D.
Founders of
THE ORDER OF CHRISTIAN MYSTICS
and
AUTHORS OF THE "CURTISS BOOKS"

2013 EDITION

REPUBLISHED FOR THE ORDER BY
MOUNT LINDEN PUBLISHING
JOHANNESBURG, SOUTH AFRICA
ISBN: 978-1-920483-22-7

Dedication

This edition is lovingly dedicated to the Memory

of the Founders of

The Order of Christian Mystics

Pyrahmos and Rahmea

and to

The Teacher of the Order

who on earth was called

Helena Petrovna Blavatsky

"Ministers of Christ and Stewards of the Mysteries of God."

1 Corinthians 4 vs. 1

TABLE OF CONTENTS

INTRODUCTION

IN presenting this volume the authors do not represent it to be a complete exposition of life in the Astral World, but only an elaboration of their lectures on the subject delivered during their transcontinental lecture tour of 1915-16, together with the lessons on the subject issued by them to the students of *The Order of Christian Mystics* during 1914-15.

To give a detailed description of the Astral World in all its phases would require quite as many volumes as a similar description of life in the Physical World. But owing to the present confused and changing conditions now manifesting on earth, during which thousands upon thousands are seeking satisfactory information on life after death, it has been deemed advisable to give the general outlines in a constructive way without waiting for leisure fully to elaborate the subject. We wish to remind such earnest seekers of the promise of Jesus: "I will not leave you comfortless, I will come unto you. . . . And I will pray the Father, and he shall give you another Comforter, that he may abide with you forever, even the Spirit of Truth. . . . Howbeit when he, the Spirit of Truth is come, he will guide you into all truth. . . . But the Comforter. . . .

he shall teach you all things and bring all things to
your remembrance, whatsoever I have said unto
you." Therefore, unless Jesus was a false teacher
it must be true that we are intended to have a
realization of the truth that life is immortal; that
the death of the body does not end all, and that a
common-sense and rational understanding of it is
ours if we will only open our hearts and let in the
Spirit of Truth which shall both comfort us and set
us free from the bonds of ignorance, misconception
and misunderstanding. For only as we do open our
hearts and correlate with the Spirit of Truth can it
open our minds, expand our preconceived ideas,
dispel our prejudices and guide us into all truth.

     In so condensed and non-controversial a presen-
tation as this must necessarily be, no effort will be
made to convince the skeptical or present elaborate arguments as to the reality of life after leaving
the physical body. It is assumed that the seeker to
whom these teachings will appeal has long since
been convinced of the survival of the personal consciousness after death and is desirous of reliable
information concerning the varied conditions in
which that consciousness functions.

     The fact of the survival of the personal conscious-
ness, with all its characteristic traits, after leaving
the physical body, we consider beyond the stage of
argument. It may seem absurd and illogical to the
untrained mind to be told that the common fluid
known as water is composed of two *gases*, oxygen

and hydrogen, in the proportion of 1 to 2. But the subject is not open to argument. It is merely a question of information as to the facts discovered, tested and proved by trained specialists in chemical research. The same is true of the problems of life after death. It is merely a question of information, not only concerning what has been taught on this subject by all great religions, spiritual teachers, philosophers, mystics and saints—the greatest minds of the race—throughout the ages, but also concerning the confirmation of those teachings which has resulted from the investigations of the keenest scientific minds of the day, men whose word is accepted as authority by the scientific world and whose mere opinion is given the greatest consideration.

While many of the teachings herein given find confirmation in the several works on psychic phenomena and after death conditions recently published, the scientists who are investigating this subject have not yet discovered *all* the facts herein explained, because they have no *all-inclusive cosmic philosophy* to guide them and because they are content to wander aimlessly in the lower regions of the Astral World where the great Spiritual Teachers are seldom if ever found. Their investigations, sincere and honest though they be, are much like laboriously searching through the plebeian sections of a great city for a scientist or professor who could explain the conditions met with, when all that would be necessary would be to take a taxi through the slums out to the university where hundreds of professors who are authorities on all branches of knowledge are to be found. Indeed, few investigators ask their way to such centers of learning or even realize that such exist in the Astral World.

As far as we are aware no previous attempt has been made to classify the various regions of the Astral World on any logical or scientific basis. We therefore endeavor to present the subject in a way that can be readily grasped, not only by students of the occult, but by the average intelligent reader.

Although there is no sharp demarcation between the Realms herein described, they are not entirely arbitrary divisions, for they follow and correspond to the seven-fold division of man and nature so well known to students.

We are well aware that there is a certain group of mental scientists, such as the followers of Hudson, Warman, etc., who consider all the manifestations of the Astral World as due to the subconscious mind, suggestion, auto-suggestion, telepathy from the living, hypnosis, etc. While we cheerfully admit the influence of all these factors, as described herein, they still leave unexplained large gaps in our knowledge of the Astral World and much of the undeniable phenomena unaccounted for.

Many such teachers oppose any exposition of the subject for fear that it will instil fear thoughts into the minds of the students, as if giving a traveller directions bow to pass in safety through the slums of a great city was inculcating in him the fear of entering it! Fear of a subject, condition or experience can be conquered, not by denying its existence or refusing to consider it, but by an accurate knowledge of its most important phases and how to master them.

Therefore, while we repeat all former warnings as to the many real dangers of investigating the Astral World without competent guidance, in this work we have endeavored to *remove all fear* of the astral from the minds of those who will give it *serious study*, by clearly setting forth the *constructive principles* whose application will master any condition encountered therein.

The teachings herein presented are not the result of psychical research as ordinarily conducted, but are the teachings on this subject given the authors by the teachers of the *Order of Christian Mystics* from the higher Realms, transmitted through Mrs. Curtiss by the *independent method* known as *theopneusty*[1] while in full waking consciousness, in collaboration with Dr. Curtiss, and verified by their personal psychic experiences in the Astral World. These teachings are therefore not a mediumistic report of the experiences of one person and his deductions therefrom, but form a *constructive philosophy* derived from Those Who Know, which has been repeatedly tested and proved reliable.

---

[1] Theopneusty is the mysterious power to hear orally the teachings or directions of a Divine Being. Theopathy is the ability to assimilate the nature of a Divine Being. Theophany is the actual appearance of a Divine Being to a mortal.

REALMS OF THE LIVING DEAD

CHAPTER I

THE REALITY OF THE ASTRAL WORLD

"Three Hails, O weary Pilgrim, lead to the end of toils, Three Hails, O conquerer of Mara, will bring thee through three states into the fourth, and thence into the seven Worlds, the worlds of Rest Eternal"

The Voice of the Silence, Blavatsky, 5-6.

THERE are so many conflicting teachings among the Christian sects as to after-death conditions and so much has been said of the allurements and dangers of the Astral World from the viewpoints of various schools of occult teaching, that we feel the teachings of *The Order of Christian Mystics* on this subject should be plainly stated, so its pupils may have a wider outlook and a clearer understanding of the subject than we have seen in the many presentations given elsewhere.

To many the very word *astral* is associated with something uncanny and dangerous, yet its literal meaning is "starry," from the Persian *Istar*, and it is still used in this sense in astronomy when referring to the stars. Its technical use in occultism, however, is in the sense of ethereal, finer or more subtle than physical matter. But on account of the frequent warnings, to many the word has become a bugaboo. In fact in some schools of occult teaching there is danger of the whole Astral World with its entities, elementals, "spooks" and its various other inhabitants, occupying in the course of time the position of the oldtime hell, devil, imps, etc. Hence, even in speaking to those who have thrown off the thrall of fear under which the world shivered in the dark for centuries, and who refuse to believe in "his majesty the devil," we must be dear and positive lest we merely continue the same fear, homage and propitiation to the old beliefs under new names.

Other schools look upon the astral as the Heaven World, and their highest aim and greatest endeavour seems to be to reach into that world for the purpose of communicating with their loved ones who, having cast off the veil of flesh, are supposed therefore to be clothed with glory and filled with omniscient knowledge and omnipotent power, able to prophesy and infallibly guide and instruct those who still remain struggling with the bonds of matter and the temptations of the flesh.

In these pages we will try to show that the position of each of the above schools is correct *to a limited extent*, yet without a cosmic philosophy which includes and gives its proper place to every phase of the astral, each standing alone is an extreme which is misleading and which is likely to lead its followers into darkness and superstition quite as dense and appalling as that of the Dark Ages.

Another school holds that because of the dangers of the astral it is best neither to investigate nor study about it until they have passed beyond it in their spiritual growth and can come back to it with full spiritual enlightenment after leaving the physical. Students who persistently hold such an idea, instead of being wide awake when they reach the astral and learning their lessons and progressing, will remain perhaps for years in a sleeping condition, dreaming about what they have conceived the Higher Realms to be. The teaching of the first school is but substituting one fear-thought for another, while the second leads to propitiation and worship of those who have cast off the dense physical body, but whose character, morals and disposition are no more changed than a man's nature and character is changed by taking off his overcoat. Such should be given the love, honor and respect which would be conceded to them on earth because of their character and ability, but no more.

Job tells us: '''The thing which I greatly feared is come upon me, and that which I was afraid of is come to me.''[1] A community swayed either by fear-thoughts or by the worship of the departed, naturally becomes intolerant and unbrotherly and such condi-

---

[1] 1 Job, iii, 25.

tions soon lead to persecution. For there is nothing so apt to make a man a bigot and sap from his nature all natural kindliness and love for his fellow man as to dwell in fear. Fear of the Astral World may easily come to occupy the place of the mediaeval fear of the devil which manifested first as a great desire to save man from the thing so greatly feared, as shown in the fiery sermons and impressive admonitions of the early church, then as a feeling of superiority over those who refuse to believe in the doctrine of a literal everlasting hell-fire, thus making a separation between those who were "saved" and those who were "lost," and finally leading by clearly defined steps to the burning of heretics and all the horrors of the Inquisition. While we wonder how such things could be, as we look back at those times, still we can recognize that they took place not because the world was passing through a necessary nightmare of horror, but as a reasonable result of the natural growth of the *seeds of fear and prejudice* sown in the hearts and minds of mankind by the barbarous gospel of eternal damnation. For if you could bring yourself really to believe that a loved one would be burned forever unless he believed as you were taught he should, you might feel justified in resorting to means revolting to your own nature to save that loved one from such an eternal punishment, even against his will or wish.

Hence it is well to pause and consider, not the enormity of the crimes of the Dark Ages, but what

led to those results, and then search carefully in
the teachings of our own day to make sure that
we are not cherishing some belief that is the child
of fear and whose fruit of intolerance is perhaps
even now leading us to condemn those who believe
differently, even though that condemnation be but
a shake of the head, a pitying look, a shrug, or as
is frequently the case, a condemnatory utterance
such as: "Those who have developed astral senses
are born diseased, and those who communicate
with the Astral World are obsessed," etc. It is also
a lack of understanding which teaches that no one
can communicate with those who have passed on
without trifling with terrible dangers; that such
communication must necessarily hold the loved
ones back in their evolution, etc. While today the
ignorance, superstition and consequent persecution
does not reach the lengths of thumb-screw and rack,
yet it is none the less hard to endure because it is
more mental and social than physical. But this must
be expected from the uncomprehending masses by
the pioneers of every advanced idea.

To understand the dangers of the second class of
beliefs, *i.e.*, that the astral and its inhabitants is the
heaven world, we again have only to glance back
over history, for these two extremes of belief are
always found side by side. Just as ignorance and
fear led to persecution, so the practice of the second
belief gradually led to black magic, witchcraft, sorcery and necromancy. A teaching or belief must be

judged *by its ultimate results*, just as a man must be judged by the life he leads. "By their fruits ye shall know them." The teachings of Christian Mysticism stand midway between these two extremes, for Truth is ever found in the center, never at either extreme.

It must be remembered that while evolution is eternal progress, the progress is spiral; also that each Race and sub-race, as evolution pushes it up the spiral Path, must reach a point directly over that at which the departure from the true teachings began, and it is at that point where it must meet the Karma of the past and face similar temptations. As a Race and sub-race we must listen to the voice of the past and learn the lessons from the degradation and suffering which sprang from the departure from the true teachings, and carefully eradicate the karmic seed which will be found sprouting in our midst, just as the seed of a weed which we thought had been killed out during the last season will be found sprouting in the same place the next season. A wise gardener will destroy the tiny shoots ere they have time to choke out the flowers. So it is with the seeds of Karma. At each new cycle we must look for the seeds of the same old weeds with which we struggled in the past and root them out, for to suffer the same things over and over would no more exhaust their Karma than for a gardener to allow the weeds to grow and choke out his crops year after year in the hope that ultimately the weeds would exhaust themselves and the flowers would triumph.

The Race is now entering upon a new cycle; is now on the spiral of evolution directly over the point where the seeds of fear and intolerance, superstition and witchcraft were planted in the former cycles. Hence the necessity for advanced students, instead of denying the existence of and turning away in fear from all things connected with the Astral World, resolutely to face them and try to gain a reasonable understanding of their many phases; the many compensations as well as the terrors, the helps and hindrances, and the great opportunities to help humanity on the part of those who understand these conditions. In short it should be realized as the Sages have always taught, that the Astral World *must be faced and conquered*, not in the sense of being destroyed, but in the sense of being annexed, colonized and ruled, just as the Physical World must be conquered, annexed and ruled ere we can truly be called masters of the land.

The first principle for the student of this subject to grasp and realize is that *the astral is a real and not an imaginary or hypothetical world*. As Sir Oliver Lodge tells us: "Though intangible and elusive, we have reason to know that Ether is substantial enough—far more substantial indeed than matter, which turns out to be a rare and filmy insertion in, or modification of the Ether of Space."[2]

Only that is real to us to which our consciousness responds. Thus when we are unconscious or dreaming

---

[2] *Raymond*, Lodge, 319

the Physical World no longer exists to us, for our senses do not respond to its vibrations. In the same way the average man is unconscious of the Astral World because his senses have not yet evolved to the point where they respond to its vibrations and report its conditions to his consciousness, yet is just as real and it exists just as surely as does the Physical World when we are unconscious of it. As man evolves, however, all his senses will gradually and normally become more and more sensitive and respond more and more perfectly to the vibrations of the Astral World, until he is as fully conscious of its various conditions and inhabitants as he is of those of the Physical World. For instance, the early races of mankind had no eyes, but in the course of evolution certain sensitive spots in the face of those primitive beings gradually developed until definite organs of sight (the eyes) were evolved. Thus it is with the opening of the astral eyes. This is the next step *after a certain stage in evolution is reached*, and everyone must reach it, whether he will or no, in due season. Each one must learn to use his senses in the Astral World and by experience learn to judge the truth or falsity of their reports just as he must learn to use his physical senses and understand their reports of the Physical World. The dangers are real, just as are the dangers of the Physical World, but they are no more to be feared than those of the physical.

The Astral World has been defined to include "all those vibrations that lie between the intensest physical activity, that is, the atomic-etheric state, and the slowest mental activity, that is, the lowest division of the world of mind." Realize then that the astral is a *material world*, although composed of matter in much finer and far more ethereal states than we find it in the Physical World; in fact so ethereal that even in its densest expression the physical senses are scarcely able to respond to its vibrations. Nevertheless the astral is a material world which exists above—in the sense of being higher in rate of vibration, the next higher octave, as well as extending far above and beyond the earth's surface—around and within the Physical World, interpenetrating every atom more completely than the air penetrates every building, receptacle or body. "The earth," therefore, as the famous venerable Bede tells us, "is an element placed in the middle of the world, as the yolk is in the middle of an egg." To understand how this finer astral matter penetrates the coarser physical matter think of a sponge lying on the ocean bed. The *water* (1st) surrounds and penetrates every fiber of the sponge. The *salts* (2nd) in the water also penetrate the sponge. A *coloring fluid* (3rd) may be added and it also penetrates the sponge. A certain amount of *air* (4th) is dissolved in the water or the fish could not breathe. This also penetrates the sponge. The *light* (5th) penetrates the water and illumines the sponge. And finally the water may be heated, and the *heat* (6th) penetrates the sponge. Thus all these outer conditions of various forms and densities of matter constitute the physical world in which the *life* (7th) of the sponge evolves and expresses itself. Just so is our physical body and its life immersed in the sea of the astral and in that sea must evolve and express itself, whether conscious or not of the exact nature and status of each surrounding element.

The astral is therefore a locality in space in relation to the Physical World, just as the ocean is a definite locality to the sponge, although completely surrounding and interpenetrating it, and of finer and more plastic matter.[3] But it is also a state of matter conditioned by an octave of vibration above the octave within which the Physical World manifests. Indeed its lower Realms are so physical that under certain conditions of condensation their inhabitants can be photographed by the ordinary camera. This is not a mere theory or even a debatable question, for the long and elaborate scientific experiments of Sir William Crooks,[4] during which the materialized astral body of Katie King was repeatedly weighed and photographed in his own laboratory, in ample light and with his own instruments, and later the experiments of the Society for Psychical Research (to whose *Annual Reports* you are referred) have long since settled the question both as to the *reality* and the *material nature* of the substance of that world. Also an electrical instrument, on the order of a telegraph instrument, devised by David Wilson, M.A., of Cambridge, England, over

---

[3] See diagrams, page 181.
[4] *Researches in Spiritualism*, Crooks. See also *Photographing the invisible*, Coates, and *Psychical Investigations*, Hill.

which he has received hundreds of independent communications in all languages, using the Morse code from those who have left the Physical World through death, definitely settles the question of the possibility of communication with the departed.[5]

Therefore since the reality and nature of the Astral World and the possibility of conscious and intelligent communication with it is no longer open to argument, being merely a question of information as to the advances of science, it behooves occult students to be familiar with the main outlines and principles of that World. But to describe it and its inhabitants in a few short chapters is quite as difficult as to describe all phases of the Physical World and its inhabitants within the same limits. It appears as variously and impresses each investigator as differently as does a city, a landscape, the mountains or the sea, and hence is described as variously. Necessarily then only the more important phases and laws can be explained in these pages.

---

[5] See *Occult Review* for June, 1917, for fuller report.

CHAPTER II

THE RIVERS OF LIFE AND DEATH

"And be showed me a pure river of water of life, clear as crystal, proceeding out of the throne of God and of the Lamb."

Revelation, xxii, 1.

BEFORE taking up the detailed description of the various divisions of the Astral World, it will be helpful to note here the general description given in our lesson *The Rivers of Life and Death*.

"One aspect of the Great Mother-force, and perhaps its lowest, is that which is called the Astral World or the astral plane, in which everything is reflected, both from the spiritual Realms above and the earth plane below. The ethereal and rarified matter of the Astral World surrounds both this globe, its humanity in general and each individual Soul just as the amniotic waters do the unborn fetus, separating them from direct contact with the higher worlds. And as the fetus floats in the amniotic waters which protect it yet separate it from direct contact with the mother and the outer world, so humanity floats in the waters of the Astral World, but unconscious of it. The amniotic waters are a secretion of the mother for the protection and nourishment of the fetus; for as they enter the digestive tract they furnish a large amount of water and nourishing albuminous substances which initiate the activities of the digestive glands and functions. But in the last few months of prenatal life these waters become contaminated with the excretions of the digestive tract and the offscourings of the body, and when absorbed these further stimulate excretion, even some hours after birth. Just so with the astral waters. While they are secreted from the Motherforce and are necessary and nourishing in their higher aspects, they also are filled with the emanations, creations and offscourings of humanity, to breathe in which — as is so often attempted through forcing psychic development before the true spiritual birth — means moral death or insanity just as surely as to breathe in the contaminated amniotic waters would mean physical death to the fetus. But sweeping through these amniotic waters, *via* the umbilical cord, is a great stream of purified blood flowing from the heart of the mother and carrying to the fetus the currents of life-force and nourishment without which its growth and development would be impossible. So through the muddy waters of the Astral World there is a great stream of spiritual life-force — to which the blood corresponds in the physical plane — direct from the heart of the Divine Mother. And unless we assimilate this force of Divine Love and build it into spiritual growth we will remain forever as spiritually undeveloped and unborn as the fetus would physically did it not assimilate the blood-stream from the mother.

"Appreciating the significance of this symbology, we see that we must indeed be 'born of water and of Spirit.' For, just as the fetus is first born into and spends its prenatal life floating in the amniotic waters, so must we be born into and be surrounded by the Astral World and imbibe its lessons—even imbibing the knowledge of some of its lower and unpleasant phases—ere we can be born into the world of Breath or Spirit. And in our undeveloped stage we float blindly, not able to cognize our surroundings and not able to breathe the true spiritual atmosphere. After the fetus has assimilated the Mother-force and reached the last stages of its prenatal development, it must begin to digest and excrete for itself ere its assimilative system is prepared to meet the conditions of individual life which prevail after birth. Just so ere our spiritual birth. We are blindly fed by the spiritual force of the great River of Life which flows through the Astral World, but there comes a time when we must imbibe for ourselves and assimilate that which is good in the waters of the astral and cast out that which we cannot utilize for our upbuilding and ongoing. In other words, our organs of spiritual digestion and elimination must be developed and begin their functions ere we are ready to meet the conditions of independent individuality in the higher Realms after our mystical new birth.

"Among the Greeks the River of Life was symbolized by the river Styx, a river of life and immortality which flowed through Acadia and emptied into the

river Acheron. The river Styx was considered the
most sacred of all rivers, so much so that Zeus, the
Father of the Gods, ordained that the most solemn
oaths of the Gods should be sworn upon it. If such
an oath were violated the forsworn had to lie in
a trance for a year and then for nine years was
debarred from the society of the Gods. The river
Acheron, on the other hand, the river into which the
Styx flowed, was regarded as the River of Death
which separates our manifested existence from the
state they called the nether world; the river of the
nether regions over which the Souls of the Dead
were ferried by the mystical boatman Charon. The
reality of this symbology is quite plain once we
remember that Acheron, the River of Death, is
the great stream of astral force which surrounds
mankind like the amniotic waters do the fetus. So
there is indeed a real River of Death—as there is
a real River of Life—over which the Souls of all
who pass out of physical life must cross. But unless
they have had their spiritual birth while still in the
physical life, they cannot cross at will but are ferried
over by the mystical boatman Charon, generally in
a state of unconsciousness which lasts for a longer
or shorter period according to their development
and their knowledge of these conditions. This is
why so many who return to communicate with
mortals from that which is called 'the other shore'
describe most graphically how they awakened upon
the shore of a great dark river whose swift current
silently flowed between them and their loved

ones, describing also the Angel of Light who bore them across. Those who have had much experience with psychic research and have communicated with those who have 'passed over the river' are amazed at the great mass of testimony which is given concerning this River and its Angel, yet as it is a very real river of force this should not be surprising. Since the literature and religion of man from the most remote ages bear the same testimony, there must be an universal principle back of the symbology, *i.e.,* the River of Death is the stream of astral force, secreted by the Great Mother, which flows around our universe as the amniotic waters do the fetus.

"In one aspect this River of Death is the river Jordan over which the Children of Israel—the Chosen of the Lord—must pass to enter the Promised Land. Physically the Jordan is a rushing, turbulent and very muddy stream, accurately symbolizing its astral counterpart. For the astral, being the great reflector, contains all the mud, debris and offscourings of earth mingled with the pure, clear Waters of Life from the spiritual plane. And those who venture into its muddy, turbulent currents without an Angelic Guide—not a mere disembodied friend or astral entity, but a Master of Light—to bear them safely over, or without the spiritual growth by which they have become consciously united to the great River of Life from their Divine Mother, are apt to be either swept away by the swirling currents or be attacked by the denizens of the Deep. Yet the law is that this River of Death must be crossed. In other words, though we may be ferried over this River many, many times from the Gate of Death, we can never pass over dry shod and enter the Promised Land until we dare to respond to the call of Joshua, The Christ-man, who commands the waters to divide, and follow Him across.

"Many will say at once, 'Have we not been warned of the dangers of entering the Astral World and of developing our psychic faculties?' To which we answer, 'Yes.' *We do not advise any effort being made* to open such faculties or any attempt made to function in the Astral World until you have become so pure of heart, so true of spirit, so faithful to your Teacher, so kind and loving that you can consciously drink of the crystal waters of the River of Life ere crossing Jordan. For these waters must become 'a well of water springing up within you into everlasting life,' and you must be able consciously to bathe in the Crystal River 'proceeding out of the throne of God,' the place where the Divine in you rules all your conditions, your life and all its activities. For there are many and terrible dangers. There are sunken rocks, covered with slime; quicksands and pools of viscous mud; there are venomous snakes and many unsightly creeping things, and there is all manner of disease and filth in this stream.

"Therefore, *we repeat all previous warnings* and say, Do not attempt to enter or cross this stream until you have the power to say to its waters, 'Divide that I may cross dry shod.' Only as you enter at the command of The Christ-man Joshua can you make all that is good and pure and helpful stand as a wall of protection and helpfulness upon your Right Hand, and all that is evil or impure to flow away on your Left Hand and out of your life, to be swallowed up in the Great Deep. You are then not attempting to cross in your own strength or at the command of curiosity or desire for sensation and psychic experiences, but are following the Ark of the Covenant in obedience to your Divine Guidance.

"Just as the intrepid mariner Odessus, who would fain cross this river and penetrate into the nether world, had to steer his ship a middle course lest, on the one hand, the alluring voice of the siren Scylla should charm his sailors (faculties) and one of her seven arms pluck them from the deck to be devoured, and on the other hand, lest his ship be sucked in and engulfed by the roaring maelstrom of Charybdis, so must the advanced student, when he has learned to master his ship of life, sail a middle course between the honeyed voice of Scylla enticing him to develop his psychic faculties and enter the Astral World of glamor and fascination, and the lure of Charybdis which will engulf his life in various forms of astral intoxication and psychic debauchery. For this is a World to be passed through under perfect control, but is not the Father's home. It is the Hall of Learning. In it thy Soul will find the blossoms of life, but under every flower a serpent coiled.[1] But essay the pas-

---

[1] *The Voice of the Silence*, Blavatsky, page 6.

sage the student must when his ship of life is captained by Odessus. In other words, we will never become truly enlightened or illumined; will never become the mystical 'Sons of God' so often referred to, with our Third Eye open, able both to see and know and understand, until some time in the course of our evolution and training, of our own free will and *without waiting for the Angel of Death* to carry us, we can walk boldly into Jordan at the command of Joshua and cross over dry shod. In Eastern scriptures the neophyte who takes this step is referred to as 'He who has entered the stream.'

"The first step in conquering this River of Death and crossing into the Promised Land is correlating your consciousness and life, not with Astral World, but with the great spiritual blood stream from the Divine Mother, the River of Water of Life. Once dipped in this stream, as Achilles was dipped in the river Styx by his mother, Thetis, and you become invulnerable to every phase of temptation and evil. And it is only by bathing your life in Divine Love and Compassion that invulnerability and immortality can ever be attained. And it is only the Divine Mother-love that can dip you into this stream of Immortal Life without overlooking the heel – the first part of the foot (understanding) to touch the Earth—as did the mother of Achilles, and enable you to conquer death.

"Strive therefore, for the Divine Love and Wisdom which shall enable you to learn your lessons out of every psychic or astral experience which the Great Law brings to you in the course of your normal development, but keep ever in mind that you are but marching through these experiences to the Promised Land."

CHAPTER III

THE SEVEN REALMS

"Without any idea of the future our existence would be purely mechanical and meaningless; with too little eye to the future—a mere living from hand to mouth—it becomes monotonous and dull"

Raymond, Lodge, 312.

JUST as the Physical World is called the "Hall of Ignorance," *i.e.,* ignorance of our Real or Spiritual Self and our spiritual destiny, so the Astral World is called the "Hall of Learning." And while the student is warned of its dangers, just as a young man is warned of the dangers of the Physical World as he leaves the shelter of the home, still only as he faces these dangers and learns to conquer them can he reach the "Hall of Wisdom," whether physical or spiritual.

In reality the dangers of the astral, although in many respects different, are no greater than the dangers of the Physical World. For instance, in using your sense of sight in the Physical World many dangers are encountered. The babe who is just beginning to use this sense is not allowed to play with hat pins, scissors or other pointed instruments lest he put his

eyes out ere he learns to use them. His eyes are
exposed to many other dangers; a speck of dirt, a
cinder, an insect may wound the eye; a condiment
such as pepper, mustard, or vinegar may be
transferred from hand to eye after eating or the eye
may be infected from the handkerchief or bit of dust.
Later in life the eyes may witness unpleasant scenes
such as filth in the gutter, dirty and disgusting men
and women, tramps, drunkards, etc., may witness
fights, accidents and disasters; may gaze on pictures
or actions which stimulate evil thoughts and animal
passions. But because of all these dangers which
the eyes must encounter, do we cover the child's
eyes with a bandage and refuse to let it develop
the function of sight because it is too dangerous?
or say that it is better for him to do without seeing
until he has grown up and can better judge how to
use it? No. Rather do the parents teach the child to
understand and judge that which it sees. The same
rule of common sense applies to the development of
the functions of our senses in the Astral World; for
the axiom, "As above so below; as below so above"
is an universal rule which applies to all Worlds.

To endeavor to skip over this World and avoid its
lessons would be to become a hothouse plant and
develop the same kind of moral and spiritual fiber
as does the young man who is brought up on the
"sheltered life" plan, unable to stand alone because
ignorant and fearful of the experiences of real life.
But just as the child should be trained in the funda-

mental principles which make for sterling character, if he is to face the dangers and conquer the temptations of the world, so must the student of occultism be trained in the application of the same principles in the higher Realms; to unswerving trust in the power of God and of The Christ within; to courage, honesty, purity of life and thought, truthfulness and fearlessness of the World he is entering. When so trained he "knows no doubtful hopes, no absurd fears, because he has no irrational beliefs: he is acquainted with the extent of his power; and he can dare without danger."[1] It is knowledge of the details of the astral which shall take away the fear of the danger of it, that we desire to expound in these pages.

In the previous chapters we found that the astral was a material world, although its higher Realms differ from its lower as much as air differs from earth. We also found that these Realms were not arbitrary divisions or mere classifications, but were separated from each other as naturally as are air, water and earth, although co-existing and inter-mingled, just as are the different forms of physical matter.

Just as the Physical World and man himself is divided by nature into seven subdivisions, according to the various forms and conditions of manifestation of which the World and man are made up, so the Astral World is naturally divided into seven subdivisions—Realms as we shall call them, for they are more than

---

[1] *Transcedental Magic*, Levi, 89.

mere sub-planes—corresponding to the seven
principles of man, in each subdivision or Realm of
which one of the seven Worlds of Manifestation is
represented and has its characteristic manifestation.
Perhaps we can get a better idea of what these
Realms are like if we go back to our simile of a
sponge and consider the water, the salt, the coloring
matter, the air, the heat, the light and the life, each
as corresponding to a separate Realm with its own
characteristics.

Each Realm is divided into seven Orders and
each Order into seven suborders.[2] This classification
is therefore not an arbitrary one, but is in harmony
with the universal seven-fold classification of the
universe. It therefore gives us a sound and scientific
basis which we may safely follow in our future
consideration and discussion of that World.

These seven Realms we have classified as follows, giving their correspondence to the Worlds of
Manifestation.

1.   *The Realm of Reflection.*
        Corresponding to the Physical World.
2.   *The Ethereal or Etheric Realm.*
        Corresponding to the Astral World.
3.   *The Realm of the Life-force or Vital Realm.*
        Corresponding to the World of the Life-
        force or Pattern World.
4.   *The Desire Realm.*
        Corresponding to the Desire World.

---

[2] See *The Voice of Isis*, Curtiss, Chapter III.

5. *The Mental Realm.*
    Corresponding to the Mental World.
6. *The Spiritual or Inspirational Realm.*
    Corresponding to the Spiritual World.
7. *The Divine or Ecstatic Realm.*
    Corresponding to the Divine World.

If we regard the Astral World as the next higher octave above the physical, its seven Realms will correspond to the same Realms or notes of the Physical World, but in a higher octave, hence will have corresponding characteristics. If this analogy is kept in mind one of the greatest stumbling blocks for the student will be eliminated. One cause for confusion is that many psychics, all who claim to understand life in the Astral World and whose testimony is hard to refute, give out contradictory reports, scarcely any two agreeing. But we would get just as differing reports if we asked a miner who spent his life under ground, a deep sea diver, a sailor, a farmer and an aviator to describe life in the Physical World as he saw it in the Realm in which he worked. *The Report depends upon the Realm or Realms to which the psychic vibrates or is attracted.*

If the psychic reaches but one Realm the others are just as non-existent as are the seven prismatic colors to one who is born color-blind or as are other musical tones to insects which respond to but one. This, together with the further illustrations given under each heading, will explain the discrepancies and conflicting statements which are so puzzling to the student. To gain a true understanding of the Astral World we must not take the statements of any one psychic, but must study the philosophy of that World under those Great Teachers who have mastered the astral as well as higher Worlds and are able to express their knowledge in a convincing and scientific manner.

Since the Astral World as a whole is the World of sensation and desire all its Realms partake of those characteristics, although greatly enhanced and intensified by the far more ethereal conditions of that World. This should be borne in mind as each Realm is studied. It should also be remembered that the World entered through the gate of death includes as many states of consciousness, and even more, than the Physical World, which is entered through the gate of birth, for birth into the Physical World is death to the Astral World, just as death to the Physical World is birth into the Astral World.

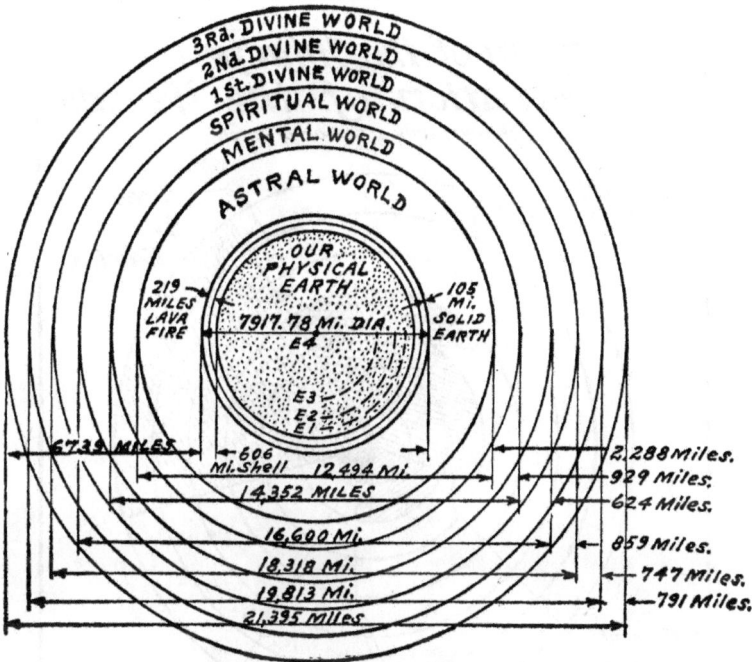

Diagram labels (from outer to inner):
3Rd. DIVINE WORLD
2Nd. DIVINE WORLD
1St. DIVINE WORLD
SPIRITUAL WORLD
MENTAL WORLD
ASTRAL WORLD
OUR PHYSICAL EARTH
7917.78 Mi. DIA.

219 MILES LAVA FIRE
105 Mi. SOLID EARTH

E4
E3
E2
E1

606 Mi. Shell
6.739 MILES
12.494 Mi.
14,352 MILES
16,600 Mi.
18,318 Mi.
19,813 Mi.
21,395 Miles

2,288 Miles.
929 Miles.
624 Miles.
859 Miles.
747 Miles.
791 Miles.

The Seven Worlds of Our Earth-chain

Every form in the visible world is but the smallest, densest and
material expression of its seven-fold manifestation. The six
expressions in the invisible worlds all surround and interpen-
etrate the physical expression as illustrated above. This applies
to man's bodies also.[1]

---

[1] For details see *The Voice of Isis*, Curtiss, 204.

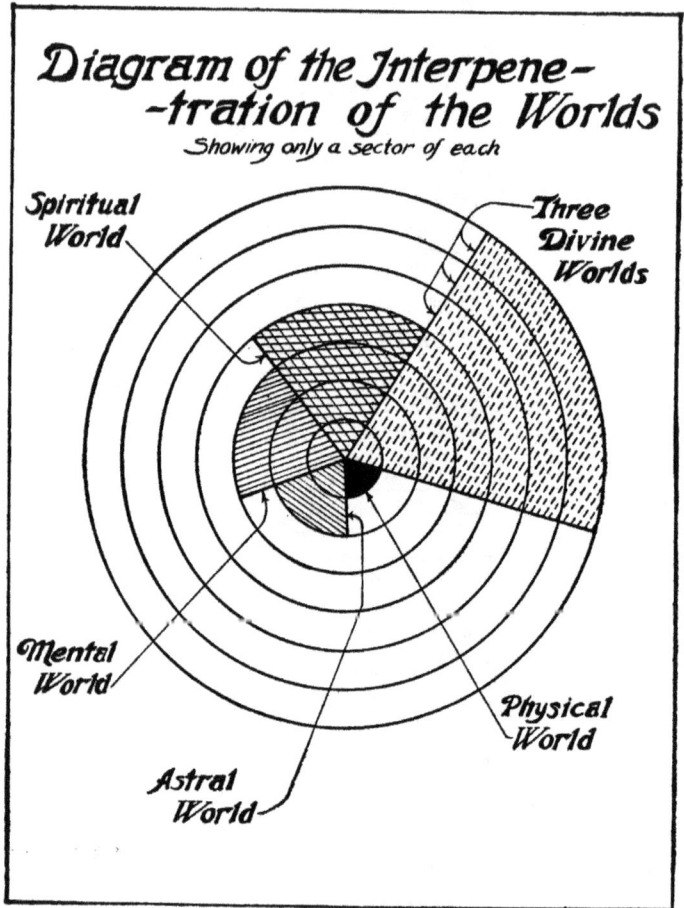

Diagram of the Interpene-
-tration of the Worlds
Showing only a sector of each

Spiritual
World

Three
Divine
Worlds

Mental
World

Physical
World

Astral
World

CHAPTER IV

THE REALM OF REFLECTION

THE SCENERY

"If freed thou would'st be from karmic chains,
seek not for thy Guru in those mayavic regions."
The Voice of the Silence, Blavatsky, 7.

"He who died at Azan sends
This to comfort all his friends;
Faithful friends! it lies, I know,
Pale and white, and cold as snow;
And ye say, 'Abdallah's dead!'
Weeping at the feet and head.
I can see your falling tears,
I can hear your sighs and prayers;

Yet I smile and whisper this,
'I am not the thing you kiss,
Cease your tears and let it lie!
It was mine, it is not I'."
After Death in Arabia, Arnold.

THE first Realm above the Physical World,
in rate of vibration, we term the *Realm of
Reflection.* Here we find reflected every object which exists in the Physical World, or to
be more accurate, the physical object—man,
animal, vegetable as well as all so-called

inanimate things—is the reflection or materialization of its astral duplicate. Here we find the astral pattern of all living things. But everything is seen reversed as in a mirror. For instance a number such as 123 would be seen as 321, etc. This fact caused the editors of Mme. Blavatsky's manuscript for *The Secret Doctrine* much labor at first when they tried to verify the quotations made by her from books presented by her Teachers to her astral vision, for she frequently forgot to reverse the number of the page.

When the editors learned this, if the quotation was not found on the page indicated, it would invariably be found on the page bearing the reversed number. This feature of the astral alone accounts for many of the mistakes of untrained psychics who are not familiar with this law.

Day and night are also the reverse of the corresponding periods on earth. Hence it is generally easier for a sensitive to contact the astral at night, although to one who is properly trained it makes little difference; for so-called night exists only in the Realm of Reflection, and Ethereal Realm and the Desire Realm. And even in these it is far from being the same as an earthly night, although the moon and stars are visible.

While the scenery of this Realm is the counterpart of the scenery of earth it is much more, for here there is a luminosity and translucence difficult to describe, which makes familiar objects far more brilliant and beautiful and reveals their true nature far more than does their physical counterpart on earth. While plants, trees, animals and people are all seen here they can also be seen through, just as on earth we can see into and through a glass of water for instance. In the Astral World we can also see all sides at once and not in perspective, and with the glow and colors imparted to everything by the currents of life-force which sweep through them. For the Astral World is a world of four dimensions instead of three. For this reason all attempts to locate the various Realms of this world in space or to limit its phenomena to our three dimensional conceptions, lead to misconception and materialization.

Wild animals, snakes, etc., are also encountered in the astral, but only in the localities corresponding to where they would naturally be found on earth. Every animal does not have a conscious life in the Astral World, as it takes many animals of one kind to express the Group Soul of a species. Hence it is only the more advanced animals that are sufficiently individualized to have an astral life. This is most common among those which have had some kind of contact with man and have absorbed more or less of his emanations of individuality. Hence it is common for all domesticated animals to be found in the astral, and even wild animals which have been hunted by man. This is one explanation of the astral tigers, elephants and other wild animals so frequently seen in India and other jungle countries. Another explanation is that the leaders of packs, herds and flocks are the most advanced, hence are usually individualized enough to have a life in the Astral World.

Here also the vegetation follows the seasonal changes of the various countries, but they occur somewhat in advance of their manifestation on earth. For that which is to manifest on earth descends from the higher Worlds into the Astral World and later is embodied on earth. We must not think, however, that it is the physical forms of objects that are thus seen, for this is not the case. As a rule physical objects are not seen from the Astral World, except during the period of dense earth attraction just after leaving the Physical World and while the consciousness is responding to the keynote of the physical more than to the astral.

Since love is the greatest attractive power, one in the astral may choose to remain in close physical contact with a loved one on earth for many years. For instance, a mother may remain so close to her children on earth that she would be able to see into their physical conditions throughout their entire lives, although she would gradually tend to see into the conditions in their hearts and minds rather than their physical conditions. There are, however, certain exceptions. By special training, analogous to that required for a mortal to see into the Astral World, one in the astral may be taught to see into the Physical World; for the astral body when purified emanates a form of radiance which under proper conditions can be projected into dense physic-

cal matter and thus make the physical visible. Also
the presence of a certain type of physical medium
enables the one in the astral to see physical objects
and persons. Otherwise the objects of the Physical
World are just as non-existent to the dweller in the
astral as are the things of the astral to the average
dweller in the physical. Those in the astral see
the astral bodies of physical objects, animals and
people, which are more or less luminous, or more
or less foggy or dense, according to their degree
of development. But since the consciousness of
those dwelling on earth is not functioning in their
astral bodies but in the physical, they appear asleep,
insensible or unresponsive to those on the astral,
except when the consciousness of the earth dweller
is responding more or less imperfectly to the Astral
World during dreams, visions, trances, etc.

The Realm of Reflection being the most objective of the Astral World, may be called the physical
aspect of the astral. The astral bodies of the great
majority of the lesser evolved humanity who have
left the Physical World therefore naturally gravitate
to this Realm. Many such so-called "spirits" report
through mediums that there is no heaven world or
perhaps, since their sensations are far more acute,
that they are worse off than when on earth, thus
showing that they are living what is little more than
an extension of their life on earth, be that life pleasant
or unpleasant. For the interests of those dwelling in
this Realm of Reflection are largely what they were

on earth and they have similar gatherings and
organizations, card-parties, clubs, churches,
theatres, recreations, etc., which attract those whose
desires affinitize them to such gatherings, each one
going just where he or she belongs by affinity.

Here also teachers and helpers from the higher
Realms descend to help and instruct those who are
seeking to understand their changed conditions and
surroundings. Many, however, are so absorbed in
the earth attractions and in trying to communicate
with their friends on earth that they will not listen or
pay any attention to such teachers, just as there are
thousands on earth who will not listen or pay any
attention to such teachings as are set forth in these
lessons, although they are accessible to all.

One feature of such help should receive special
mention. There is an organization in the higher
Realms similar to the Red Cross Society which
has workers whose duty it is to descend into this
lower Realm to aid, care for, comfort and instruct
those who are passing out, especially those who
know something about the change and are willing
to listen and receive instruction. This organization
is specially equipped to watch over, help and instruct those who are passing out in great numbers in
times of disaster, pestilence and war; indeed many
soldiers as soon as they are fully awakened to the astral conditions are enlisted in this astral Ambulance
Corps, and most of them eagerly give their services,
under the able instruction of appointed teachers,
until they can be taught no longer to identify

themselves with earth conditions. Those who will not profit by instruction must be left, just as such must be left on earth, to learn through experience, perhaps by suffering, if they will not learn without it.

Those who know of these helpers can therefore be met and be taken care of, students of this Order being met by members of the Order over there acting under the direction of the Teacher of the Order. They can also arrange for their loved ones to be met by a reception committee which will include the dear ones who have gone before, provided they are still interested in those left behind and naturally wish to welcome them. Such a reception is by no means confined to members of the Order of Christian Mystics, for all that is necessary for anyone in any part of the world is to send out a mental wireless call for the invisible helpers and the loved ones will be gathered to greet the newcomer. These facts are the basis for the belief in the efficacy of prayers for the dead—purgatory being simply the lower Realm of the Astral World—also for the belief in the value of baptism for the dead as advocated by St. Paul,[1] for not only do such prayers surround the loved one with comforting, helpful and protective thought forces, but they also serve to call the attention of the invisible helpers to their needs. Therefore if in the course of your development you should contact a departed one who needs help, instead of allowing him to throw his condi-

---

[1] *I Cor.*, xv, 29.

tion over you or control you, *mentally* tell him to
call for helpers and seek the Light, and that if he
desires to communicate with you he must stand
some distance away and communicate mentally in
the manner we shall describe when we take up the
Mental Realm.[2]

A great work could be done by Spiritualists who
attend seances if, instead of seeking merely for
personal messages for themselves from those who
have passed over, they made a point of explaining
to all who visited them from the astral, that a cry for
help and Light would at any time bring to them one
of the teachers who could and would joyfully help
them. There are many earnest and loving persons
who do this and aid many Souls in the astral to find
help and comfort. But on the other hand at almost
every séance there will be one or more wandering
Souls seeking aimlessly for their friends and relatives left behind, because they feel they must renew
the old relationship, knowing naught of any other.
Children are often heard crying for a mother, also
mothers seeking their children, and if the relative
happens not to be known by the sitters, how often
selfish and heartless remarks are made, such, for
instance, as "No one here knows your child, so pass
on," when one word of help would mean so much.

It should be clearly understood that no one is
confined to this Realm of Reflection except by the
density of his astral body and the earthliness of his
thoughts and desires, just as no one is confined to

[2] See page 179.

materialistic thoughts while on earth unless he so desires. For in this Realm a cry or even a strong desire for Light and help will bring it.

While the astral body is still dense and heavy with the water vapor, gases and magnetism of earth, the recently deceased person is apt to think he can be transported only by walking, running or riding in conveyances. He therefore walks or rides either in the astral counterpart of such vehicles or in the thought-forms of them created either by himself or collectively by all who think they need such vehicles. Later on they learn that so little energy is required that the astral body can be transported by the will, a strong thought of or desire to be in a certain place transporting it there almost immediately. Although there is usually a sense of a definite journey through the air. During such incredibly swift passages the emanations of their auras stream out behind them and are often mistaken for wings by untrained psychics. Many mortals dream of flying through the air because they remember such journeys made in the astral during sleep or because they remember such experiences during their excarnate existence previous to their present incarnation.

The recently deceased thinks he can be nourished only by the same kinds of food which were necessary for his physical body. In fact the glamor of this Realm makes him think that he must carry on life just as he did while on earth and subject to the same laws, and it may be a long time before he learns better. Hence, many of the more ignorant and less advanced, as well as the "high livers" and the gluttonous are found thronging the kitchens of hotels and restaurants and sucking in the vapors and emanations from the food that is being cooked, as do many others in the kitchens of their former homes. The more intelligent are able to draw to themselves duplicates of their favorite dishes, the creative power of their thought forming them not as mere illusions, but from the astral emanations of the physical substances. For while the astral body still contains so much dense earth magnetism and matter the need is still felt for some form—even if it be only the less material—of physical food.

The law of specific gravity obtains here as well as in the Physical World; just as a physical object or body will sink or float according to its density, so the astral body will sink into the denser strata or will float up into the particular stratum and Realm to which it is affinitized. We are told "As a man thinketh in his heart so is he," and in the Astral World this fact becomes very apparent. Here we literally find ourselves in the environment our thoughts had created while on earth, with the same kindred Souls and living out the true inmost thoughts and desires of our heart which perhaps on earth we had tried to hide, for here there is no cloak to hide our true inner desires. As we think, so are we. Therefore to some it is hell, to some but an extension of earth life, while just as surely to others it seems to be Heaven. Both these regions will be dealt with more fully later on.

The more degraded haunt barrooms and brothels in an effort still to experience the desired sensations. (This phase will be treated more fully when we describe the Desire Realm.) But as the denser atoms fall away and the earth attraction loses its power the person finds that in some mysterious way he is transported through the air wherever in thought he desires or wills to be, and is nourished by currents of force brought to him by the mere thought of food, and still later he forgets all about the necessity for food.

While the astral body may remain for a long time in this Realm the consciousness can soar into the higher Realms at any time, provided the *desire to reach up* is present, just as with those still on earth the consciousness can leave business and household cares and soar into the realms of literature, art, science or spiritual thought. In other words, *desire is the governing factor* in the Astral World even more fully than on earth. But in this more ethereal World the desire promptly brings the condition desired, while on earth its attainment is hampered and delayed by the limitations of the more dense and rigid matter which must be overcome ere it can manifest.

The substance of the Astral World is so ethereal that it is moulded by thought, hence any entity who understands the mechanism can assume any appearance it desires, even that of an angel of light, as St. Paul tells us.[3] For instance, it is quite common for

---

[3] *II Cor.*, xi, 14.

excarnate entities to copy the appearance and ape the manners of some great personage, and to appear to sitters at a séance under high sounding names, generally claiming to be great teachers and endeavoring to gain the confidence of their dupes and ultimate victims through flattery, lust or promises of great attainments or rewards to be granted if they give implicit obedience to them, or more commonly to tell them of some great and important work which they can only accomplish through the help of the entities. Therefore beware of any entity, voice or guide who tells you how great you are, were or are *about to become*, or who offers you great reward, or who suggests to you that some one is your "soul-mate" and that with this person's help you can do great things, or who fires your imagination and stimulates your passion by giving you vague and insinuating hints of a lover, soul-mate or affinity, or some other romantic relation; for all such are seeking to enter your aura over the line of flattery, greed or desire, that they may sap your vital life-force and use you as an instrument to gratify their own desires.

Again, elementals or spirits take possession of a cast-off astral body and animate it with a semblance of life and appear to a sitter as his father, mother or some loved one whom they are impersonating. This fraud can easily be detected, however, for such an one although cunning, has but a modicum of reflected human intelligence and can seldom go further than to repeat events or phrases still pictured in the brain of the cast-off astral body, or to repeat some catch phrases used by the medium such as, "I am happy and progressing," and if asked: "How is Mary?" will say: "Mary is progressing, good-bye." For it must be remembered that the Astral World is a World of illusion, and just as we find many on earth trying to be something much greater and more important than they really are, so in this World they endeavor to gain importance and a following of dupes on the physical plane by claiming to be other than themselves. It is only dupes in the Physical World, however, whom they deceive, since in the Astral World, as we have explained, it is possible to see through as well as around things and people, hence their true nature is plainly discerned.

Such elementals or entities, if given power through recognition, propitiation or obedience, imbibe sufficient human mind stuff from their followers to make themselves more or less intelligent in a cunning sort of way and often acquire great power over their victims. No one need have any fear of such entities, however, for two reasons: First, one will seldom encounter such entities unless he affinitizes with them, hence attracts them to him or unless he seeks them out, just as he would seldom come into contact with drunkards, criminals and degenerates on earth unless he deliberately entered their habitat. In the astral as in the physical, you seek the association of those with whom you affinitize. Second and most important, no one should fear the entities of the astral because they can always be controlled or driven away by the invocation of Spiritual Light, either through prayer, a challenge as to their identity "In the Name of the Living Christ" or a determined demand for Truth, such as we will give more fully elsewhere.

This does not mean that you should send out a challenge of defiance to everything in the astral, for there are entities of great power and malignance which it would be very foolish to arouse or invite to combat. But it does mean that you have a sure means of protection against anything you may encounter in the course of your *normal* development. All messages received from the departed must be received with the same good common sense and be judged by the same standards that you would use in dealing with the world; indeed even greater caution must be used since the glamour and delusion of this Realm is more difficult to resist, yet good sense, and a firm trust in the power and protection of the Christ within can make you fearless and able to cope with all its deceptions. "In it thy soul will find blossoms of life, but under every flower a serpent coiled."[4]

Here also are found the astral graveyards where the discarded astral bodies are gathered.[5]

---

[4] *The Voice of the Silence*, Blavatsky, 6.
[5] Pupils who are still on earth sometimes wander into such regions while out in the astral, just as they might wander into a physical graveyard, and are often badly frightened by the ghastly sights encountered, but a strong thought will immediately carry them up through or away from such regions.

THE ASTRAL DOUBLE

"As a man throweth away old garments and putteth on new, even so the dweller in the body, having quitted its old mortal frame, entereth into others which are new."

Bhagavad Gita.

IN the case of both man and the animals their astral pattern is not directly related to the physical body, but projects from itself a shadowy counterpart called the astral double. This double is capable of infinite contraction so as to be contained in the fetus and become the basis of the physical manifestation. The growth of the fetus simply abstracts the physical elements from the mother and builds them into the meshes of the astral double, thus materializing it. This double is not only the model into the meshes of which the physical is built, but it is also the vehicle by means of which the currents of lifeforce from the astral body, which is always in the Astral World, as well as the life-force liberated by the digestion of food and derived from the water and air, reaches and supports the physical body. "It is the reservoir or sponge of life, gathering it up from all the natural kingdoms around, and is the intermediary between the kingdoms of Pranic and physical life.[1] . . . . Life cannot come immediately from the subjective to the objective, for Nature goes gradually through each sphere. Therefore the astral body is the intermediary between the vital world and our physical body, and pumps in the life."[2] It is also the vehicle by which the vibrations of the Physical World reach the consciousness of man as sensations. The lower kingdoms whose evolution has not as yet built up the body of sensation, or only in a rudimentary way, are more directly connected with the astral double.

The above explains why all forms of life cease to grow in size when the astral double has been materialized to its full size, for then no further increase in size can take place. In cases of myxedema or giantism when the body continues to grow enormous feet and hands or to a height of seven or eight feet, the continued growth is due to a defect in or disease of the astral centers governing growth, a condition which can frequently be cured by remedies affecting those centers, especially the thyroid gland, the hypophysis cerebri, etc.

Death is therefore simply the withdrawal of this finer astral double and its contained life-force from the physical shell. It is the withdrawal of this definite

---

[1] See page 99.
[2] *The Secret Doctrine*, Blavatsky, iii, 593.

body that gives to the outer body that is left behind the shrunken and cadaverous appearance seen in so called death. This also accounts for the loss in weight of the physical body immediately after death and before evaporation could account for such loss. Physical scientists who have investigated this subject claim that the ounce or two loss in weight represents the weight of the "soul," whereas it is simply the weight of the dense astral double that is missing. This astral double is attached to the physical body by an astral cord something like an umbilical cord, which does not permit it to withdraw very far from the physical, although in some mediums it can be extruded to a considerable distance and be used as the basis for materializations. Normally at death it should be indrawn into the astral body proper, although it is often left floating near the physical corpse, and in certain atmospheric conditions it can be seen objectively by the physical sight as a wraith or "ghost."

Since the astral body is the counterpart of the physical, when it is withdrawn from the physical, it bears the exact likeness of the mortal, with all the distinguishing marks, moles, etc., it possessed at the time of transition. Those who have passed on into the astral are therefore as easily recognized and identified as they would be on earth. For, as we have said repeatedly, after leaving the physical body, there is little more change of appearance than there is in a mortal when he removes his overcoat, except that when a physical limb or part is lost the astral part will not be lost, unless so shown for purposes of identification.

After passing on from a long and exhausting illness, and especially in the case of an old person who is tired of life and no longer clings to it by either thought or desire, it is common for such a one to pass into a deep and restful sleep varying in duration according to the individual needs, previous ideas, etc. We know, of course, that thought and desire rule the Physical World, but in the Astral World they rule to a far greater degree and far more quickly, for the plastic matter of that World yields very rapidly to the creative and moulding power of thought and will. Therefore a person who for years held the thought that leaving the Physical World ended all, or one who believed that he would sleep until Gabriel blew his trumpet, would naturally pass into a comatose or dense sleeping condition after passing on. This condition would perhaps last for years or even centuries, until the desire or thought force put into the idea was exhausted and he was released from its effects.

All these types of sleepers float aimlessly in the Astral World, swept hither and thither by astral currents which, much like the winds of earth, are continually flowing in various directions; for it must be remembered that in this Realm we can see as well as feel these astral winds. And as the astral is the World of Desire and Sensation, we can here see

that many of these winds are but the forces
generated by man's restless and disquieting
thoughts which form mighty currents plainly seen
to be made up of living elementals, tenuous forms
even in this Realm, yet passing in great streams
and with a moaning cry, much as the wind moans
on earth. Again there can be seen mighty storm-
winds made up of the embodied evil and malignant
thought forces generated by mankind, here seen
entitized as demons of destruction sweeping on
with tremendous power. Yet always there is blowing
here a steady wind from the East which is the force
of blessing sent forth into all the world from the
Heart of the Universe. This appears as made up of
Angelic Beings who float on with faces radiant,
unseeing and unheeding anything through which
they pass, intent only on their mission, which is to
carry the divine creative love-forces and pour them
out on all creation. The sleeping and floating forms
are therefore in danger as well as very much in the
way, quite as much so as would one be on earth who
lay down in a busy thoroughfare and went to sleep.
Therefore special attention is given to such, very
much as special policemen would prevent a like
occurrence on earth; there are those whose business
it is to look after such Souls, and to convey them to
specially prepared retreats where they are tenderly
cared for and protected.

This among many other tasks is the work assigned
to those students who during sleep on earth have

asked to be put to work in the Astral World. Many of
us would be surprised could we remember the tasks
we performed during sleep; for we do not spend all
our time at the Masters' feet drinking in wisdom,
although we do receive teachings according to
our needs and desires. Those who sincerely wish
to learn are taught through experience the great
lesson of humility by learning to perform gladly
the most menial tasks, and in time the quantities
of sympathy for the helpless, willingness to help
without seeming recognition, and the humility
needed to do the little things, are inculcated in our
Souls and later begin to manifest in our lives. Then,
and then only, are we assigned to more important
tasks.

Those who wake up immediately or soon after
passing on, usually have a short period of confusion
while they are getting their bearings, much as one is
sometimes confused on awaking in a dimly lighted
room which seems full of vague shadows until one
is fully awake and recognizes things as they are.
To many this transitory condition inspires fear, especially if they passed on with a fear of death. But
with the help of their loved ones or others duly appointed by the Masters, this fear soon passes and
they realize what the change is that has taken place.
The thing to impress upon the minds of all is, that
the moment a Soul cries out for Light and help, at
that moment help is sent. And when one is passing
through the change called death, if the friends and
relatives send up the prayer of faith that the Soul

shall be met on the threshold of the other world, it will be done. Especially is this true of those who either belong to this Order or who have friends or loved ones who are about to pass over. If they write to this Center and request help, some of the many in the Astral World who are trained and taught and organized for this purpose will prepare for the coming Soul, much as the birth of an infant on the earth is prepared for. They will also notify the personal friends of the ones passing over to meet them, and will see to it that if such a one sleeps for even a long time, he will nevertheless be watched over and protected, so that when he does awaken there will be some loving face to allay even a momentary pang of loneliness or fear, and to explain to him the nature of the new conditions of life.

Many, however, are not welcomed owing to the fear inspired by their false earthly teaching. For instance, we have known a wife who solemnly enjoined her husband as he was passing on, "Don't you dare to come back around me." At her passing on, karmic law would not permit him to know of it or to meet her. Those who are not thus met naturally do not know where they are or why they are surrounded by such unfamiliar conditions, or they may for a time think they are dreaming. They may remember that they have been sick but think they have just waked up from a night's sleep.

Others when they awaken to the fact that they are not really dead but are as much alive as ever, cannot believe they have crossed the great river[3] and entered another state of existence. As they have considerable physical force and magnetism clinging to them they are naturally in very close relation with the friends they have left behind; can still see them moving about preparing for the funeral of the body of flesh they have so recently quitted, but refusing to speak or pay attention to them. While in this sphere of attraction they are acutely sensitive to the emotions of those to whom they are so closely connected, magnetically as well as mentally. Hence the weeping and display of grief so often indulged in by the mourners causes the departed ones great anguish and suffering, as emotions of grief, sorrow or inharmony cause greater suffering and have a far more depleting and exhausting effect upon the astral body than upon the physical body, great as we know that to be. Especially is this so when the departed ones are unable to make the loved ones understand that they are not dead, only gone on before; cannot make them realize their presence, their love and their solicitude over the conditions and changes transpiring on earth. Therefore as little emotion as possible should be displayed over the passing of a loved one, specially at the time of the passing when everything should be peaceful and calm, and for the first few days afterward while the loved one is still closely enmeshed in earth conditions. Particularly

---

[3] See page 30.

this is true of those who pass out through accident while in the full vigor of life. Such persons still have so much physical life-force and magnetism in their auras that they remain in close touch with earth conditions for long periods, at least as long as they would normally have lived but for the accident.

We should say farewell to our loved ones with no more grief than would be natural were they starting on a long journey on which they would be absent a number of years, for we will see them again, when we follow them, just as surely as on earth if we journeyed to their new home. Instead of spending time and force in useless grief and mourning the time should be spent in quiet meditation and in an effort to correlate our consciousness with theirs and assure them of our love and understanding. Mourning clothing should not be worn nor should constant visits be paid to the grave, for all such acts and thoughts *tend to hold the departed one down to the discarded body* through the law of attraction.

The recently deceased is often strongly, even morbidly attracted to the discarded physical body for some time, hence haunts its burial place. But it is thus held only as a result of thought or desire, the desire to see what becomes of the former outer garment it wore while on earth. Cremation is therefore always desirable, not only because more sanitary and less revolting to think of, but because it consumes the physical magnetism and this releases the deceased at once from that source of attraction to the Physical

World. But great care should be taken to see that cremation is not carried out until the astral body has had time to withdraw completely from the physical body or considerable suffering to the departed one may result. Several of those whose bodies have thus been cremated somewhat prematurely have complained to us and requested that we give the above warning in our teachings. Another reason for delay is to be sure that the person has really left the body *permanently* and not temporarily, as in a state of catalepsy, trance, etc. The best indication as to the proper time for cremation is when definite signs of physical disintegration appears. The attending physician should be requested not to sign the death certificate or permit embalming until these signs appear or until a trained and reliable psychic is able definitely to assert that the Soul has completely left the body.

CHAPTER VI

THE AWAKENING

"Sweet friends: what the women lave
For the last sleep of the grave,
Is a hut which I am quitting,
Is a garment no more fitting,
Is a cage from which at last,
Like a bird, my soul hath passed.
Love the inmate not the room,
The wearer not the garb—the plume
Of eagle, not the bars
That kept him from those splendid stars."
                After Death in Arabia, Arnold.

IN the case of the majority of persons, the first emotion on awakening in the Astral World is an intense and weird loneliness, a confused consciousness of being surrounded by vague shadowy forms, and of being watched by innumerable eyes, yet without the ability fully to formulate their thoughts or understand by whom or what they are watched. For at this stage the awakened ones have not yet learned to use their astral senses or to discriminate among the strange sights, sounds and feelings. It must be remembered that in the Astral World for a time they are in the same relative position as is a new-born babe when it first opens its eyes to earth life. Could we enter into the babe's feelings we would find vague memories of the life it had left, a sense of just awakening from a deep sleep (the period of gestation) and a newborn and uncomprehending wonder at the strange sights and sounds surrounding it. If, however, the ones passing over have studied or have had at least some understanding of what they are to expect, the confusion is but momentary. And if they have prepared for the change by having some wise Soul gather together their loved friends and relatives to meet them, it is a joyous reunion.

In the case of sudden death, either by accident or in the war, when the mind is filled with the desire for life and the intense excitement of battle, the first awakening often brings the soldiers a sense of being suddenly awakened after having fallen asleep at their posts, and they look around in amazement for the familiar battlefield. The great stillness after the roar of battle strikes terror to their Souls. Then perhaps a bird can be heard singing joyously near them—for physical sounds can be heard in the astral—until its singing melts their hearts and perhaps a flood of tears brings relief. Even those who have passed out in hatred, with the lust for killing strong within them, awaken in this great silence and loneliness only to find no one near them. In both instances this is purposely arranged, so that whatever is good in them may have a chance to awaken.

Especially is this true in the case of those who

pass out through an explosion or who have been victims of a bursting shell, in which case the astral as well as the physical body has been shattered. In such a case it will take some time ere the attractive and cohesive power of the life-principle can draw the astral atoms around it and reconstruct the bodily form. During this period the Soul remains unconscious. In such a case the feeling on first awakening will be quite similar to the sensations of returning consciousness after an anesthetic, the same feeling of faintness and exhaustion, which, however, soon passes off.

Many, after passing through the first period of silence and great loneliness, when they first begin to recognize others around them, even one whom on earth they would have called an enemy, are so glad to find companionship that, be they on their side or the enemy's, they are eagerly sought; for at this stage it is the attitude of the real Inner Man that is apparent, hence those of similar natures and ideals are instinctively attracted, no matter what their positions may have been on earth. Only as they begin to identify themselves with their old earthly conditions, with the old personality, its uniform, equipment, last orders, etc., do they realize the difference in nationality. With some few however, the force of the old hostilities and thoughts may for a time impel them to hunt out and attack the enemy. In such cases they at once, through their strong thought-force, return to the battlefield on the physi-

cal plane, but on there they find conditions greatly
changed.

When in the flesh it was quite easy to know on
which side they were fighting; friend and foe could
be distinguished merely by their uniforms, but now
all is different, for to the astral sight the real forces
back of the war (good and evil) are plainly seen,
and the aura of each man who is truly and heroically
fighting for principle, even though mistaken, is illumined by the light of his ideals, the light varying
in color and brilliancy according to the strength
and purity of these ideals. While over each one
filled only with cruelty, hatred and the desire to
kill—a sort of blood madness—can be seen hosts
of the most malignant entitized forces, *i.e.*, forces
manifesting in forms which express the thoughts of
evil which generated them. These forms are seen to
surround their victims, sometimes like monstrous
serpents, which writhe in and out of their bodies,
emerging from the heart or solar plexus or again
from the mouth or head. And over all may be seen
clouds of evil faces; forms of unspeakable cruelty
and lasciviousness horribly pictured in living but
unearthly shapes. If the Soul belongs to the side of
evil he will join his forces with these monsters in
orgies of horror and throw himself madly into the
fray, becoming in turn, because of his disembodi-
ment, an obsessing demon. If, however, he has in
him even a spark of better feeling (and how few are
entirely without it) sooner or later he allies himself
on the side of good.

But there are thousands of helpers on the battle fields and in the trenches trying to help all who will listen, to realize their real condition and what they are really fighting against. They are thus gradually taught that it is not their fellow men they should attack, but *the evil forces that are obsessing certain leaders of the Central Powers* and trying to obsess the rank and file as well, playing upon and enlarging and driving to extreme expression every animal and brutal instinct and selfish desire which become like open doors through which such forces can manifest. All the lust-forms and demons which are the inciting causes of the war are there seen in their true and hideous form, the personified forms of lust, hate, greed, cruelty, ambition, desire for power, etc. These evil entities are seen to swarm around and mingle in among the fighters on both sides and urge them to give vent to cruelty and their baser passions. But as we have seen, they are successful only with those whose minds are open and receptive to such incitements. Therefore hundreds of thousands of soldiers in the astral, gathered from both sides of the conflict, are fighting side by side to destroy the obsessing demons. In fact, many of the soldiers from the Central Powers, seeing how their former leaders and comrades are obsessed by these swirling vortices of evil force, are the most eager, energetic and courageous of all—for it takes courage of a high moral as well as physical quality to encounter these vaporous, clammy whirlpools of evil

—in their efforts to destroy them and free their people from their influence. Especially is this true of those illiterate portions of central Europe where witchcraft and black magic have been practised for ages, and whose inhabitants are especially susceptible to such influences.

Those in the astral who keep trying to fight are only those few who have made themselves channels through which the evil astral forces could express and who would be so filled with hatred and lust of battle that they would desire to continue after passing on, just as it is only the comparative few out of the great mass of mankind who desire to continue their habits of debauchery after passing on.

As we said in *The Philosophy of War*[1] the real instigators of this war are the evil astral forces, "the hosts of the accumulated thought-forms of lust, greed, envy, hate, selfishness and unbrotherliness engendered by the wrong thinking of humanity from the beginning, as well as the results of their evil words and deeds, all of which are ever seeking expression through their creators. . . . During this battle all the stored up evil must have a focus through which it can pour itself out upon the lowest or physical plane where its precipitation will end the cycle of its manifestation, adjust the Karma and permit the good aspect of the forces involved to be extracted."

"Germany . . . through ambition, pride and

---

[1] Page 26-7.

lust for power has opened the door to the hordes of evil astral forces which are seeking to obsess humanity and wreck their will upon it. Hence, through giving expression to these forces, Germany has become the instrument through which they are being poured out into the world to the testing of the other nations, just as Judas became the instrument of testing to the other disciples."

CHAPTER VII

ASTRAL HELPERS

"Death is not a word to fear, any more than birth is. We change our state at birth, and come into the world of air and sense and myriad existence; we change our state at death and enter a region of what?"

Raymond, Lodge.

IN the Physical World we are able to mould or shape the matter of this world according to our thought, but it requires special instruments such as knives, saws, chisels, etc., or special processes such as dissolving or melting the materials and pouring them into specially prepared moulds, etc. But the material of the Astral World is so plastic that it is moulded by thought-force and will. Hence all that is necessary in that World is to think intently of the thing desired and it will soon appear. It will be perfect and beautiful in proportion as the thought held is clear, definite and perfect, or will be hazy and imperfect as the thought is not clear or is allowed to wander. The thing desired will also appear quickly or slowly according as the will and desire for it is strong or weak. For forms in the Astral

World seem to the astral sight as solid and substantial as do the forms on earth to our physical sight, although we know that the particles of such physical forms are separated by relatively large spaces. A person in the lower Realms of the astral can even pinch himself and feel the substantial flesh or injure himself by being struck by an astral object. In fact the astral body can be wounded, not only by astral weapons, but by physical instruments with sharp points or cutting edges. "When swords are struck at shades, it is the sword itself, not its Astral, that cuts. Sharp instruments alone can penetrate Astral, *e.g.*, under water a blow will not affect you, but a cut will."[1] This is one reason why swords crossed above a bed have for ages been considered a protection against astral entities. No blood flows from such wounds, but for a short time the life-force may be seen oozing out as a lavender mist.

Astral forms and objects, when seen by the living but untrained clairvoyant, might seem most shadowy and unsubstantial. And were a mortal to try to touch such objects with his physical hand it would pass through them quite as readily as they pass through physical objects. On the other hand, physical objects when seen from the Astral World are quite as shadowy or transparent.

Those who lose limbs or other parts of the body through war, accident or surgical operations find them fully restored in the astral, although for a

---

[1] *The Secret Doctrine*, Blavatsky, III, 589.

time their old habits of thought may make them seem still lacking if it has been some time since their loss. Long continued thought of the loss of a limb gradually atrophies the astral double, but after passing on, when the thought pressure is removed, the life-force rapidly flows in and the limb soon fills out. When they first pass into the astral the missing limb seems to be but a mist or vapor, hence is not recognized. But this atrophied vapory limb gradually solidifies until the limb is as perfect as the rest of the body. If the limb or organ has only recently been lost its astral double will be quickly recognized.

The things created in the astral are thus not mere figments of the imagination or mere thought-forms, but are thought-forms which have descended into the Astral World from the Mental World and have attracted to themselves the emanations of corresponding things on earth. Thus the astral and finer physical substances released and thrown off from their forms by the ever-changing process of life and also by the greater disintegrating process of decay ascend into the astral and are embodied either into corresponding astral forms or are used in giving astral substantiality to other astral creations.

Everything is created by thought and desire. For instance, on first passing over the Soul appears in the clothing he last remembered having put on; for the thought-forms of his whole wardrobe are at hand, ready to take on astral substantiality by the creative power of his thought. There are also shops and factories where anything the person thinks he must have can be obtained.

Elementals created by thought and embodied in astral matter are often built up into artificial but powerful tribal deities and worshipped as such by the lower types of savages, and such entities will fight and work for those who serve them. To obtain greater power to accomplish *physical* results on earth such tribal elementals often require the physical life-force liberated by the shedding of blood, hence demand the blood sacrifice of some animal or even a human being. Such entities are not "spirits" in the sense of angels or the higher spiritual beings usually referred to by that term, nor are they even disembodied mortals, but are entirely non-human except in so far as they have been endowed with low cunning or intellect and other human qualities by the streams of thought-force and other emanations of their devotees. It is the communion with and worship of such non-human entities that constitutes "spiritism" and necromancy as distinguished from "Spiritualism," the latter referring to communion with the human and super human residents of the Astral World. There is nothing spiritual, only devilish, about the first process, while the latter is highly spiritual, in spite of many exceptions among those who seek only for physical phenomena and care little for their own moral and spiritual development.

Wherever blood is shed a certain class of elementals

is attracted, for as they are seeking advanced and ultimate human embodiment they seek to imbibe the life-force from the blood of higher forms of life, especially the human. Hence all surgical operations should be preceded by prayer or invocation and the patient should be surrounded by the protecting thoughts of his friends during the operation. When this is not done elementals frequently enter his aura, increasing the liability to infection, through depleting the vitality, and even causing infection through precipitating astral infections into the wound. Or they may attach themselves to him as vampires, sap his vitality and retard or even prevent recovery. In many cases in which these or similar directions have been followed the recovery has been astonishingly rapid and complete, the time required in many cases being less than half the usual. Some surgeons and physicians naturally have this protecting power, hence while no more skilful than others, their percentage of recoveries is much greater than that of their colleagues, especially after having received these instructions from the Order and consciously controlling the conditions.

Students of the O. C. M. who are about to un-dergo serious operations can be met in the Astral World, as they pass out of the body under the an-esthetic, by a special band of trained workers and nurses who will take care of them and protect their physical body while it is being operated on, if they will notify the Secretary of the Order in time, either by letter or telegram and at the same time send out a mental call for the Teacher and helpers of the Order in the higher Realms. If there is no time to notify the Secretary the mental call for help and protection will bring it. Of course such help and protection are not confined to members of the Order but the Order has a special organization for that purpose. We have many letters on the file testifying to the practical nature of such help, both from the surgeons and the patients themselves.

If no attempt is made to take care of patients at such a time, they tend to wait around near the body, often remaining so close to the physical that they suffer severe nervous shock, or agonies of fear if they see the operation from the astral. This fear always adds to the dangers, retards recovery and even though apparently forgotten lives in the subconscious mind as a vague horror for the rest of their lives. Hence the Importance of being taken care of during the operation and receiving psychic and spiritual help during convalescence.

Also at such times it is quite possible for the Soul to be taken far above the physical, even into the presence of the Masters, and to receive helpful instruction which, even though seemingly forgotten on awakening from the anesthetic, will still have its influence on their lives or come to them as a memory at some future day.

Since the American Indians are very closely af-finitized to the earth it is in this Realm where most of them remain and pursue their desires in this "Happy Hunting Ground." The Christian Mystic Philosophy teaches that each human being has its soul-home on the planet from whose spiritual Hierarchy it emanated.[2] As the soul-home of the Indians is on this planet they are properly called "earth children." They are so affinitized to the soul of the earth that they can correlate more perfectly with its forces, hence after they pass on they can bring a great deal of vital force and healing magnetism to those in touch with them. This is one of the reasons for the many cures wrought through their aid.

Naturally therefore the Indians are usually the first ones to be encountered by one who is beginning to develop his astral senses. We, therefore, find that nearly all subjective mediums who "go under control" have an Indian for a "guide" and have Indians in their "spirit band." These Indians are by no means the lowest dwellers in the Astral World, but are simply the nearest to the Physical World. They are usually kind-hearted and desirous of helping their mediums to the best of their ability and do not know that their *method* of helping and guiding, *i.e.,* descending into the medium's body to control it, is a wrong and *degenerating method*, both to themselves and to the medium. They are in striking contrast to that undesirable and most dangerous class of entities the voodoo workers, sorcerers and black

---

[2] See *The Voice of Isis*, Curtiss, 187-8.

magicians of various savage tribes who have passed
into the astral and desire to secure followers and
pupils to perpetuate their rites and practices. But as
said above, these are not likely to be contacted by
the white people of civilized nations unless sought
for.

In this Realm also wander the "earth-bound spirits" or those who are bound close to earth by some
great and overwhelming desire such as revenge
for having been murdered; the miser's love for his
gold; the youth's desire for physical life, etc. Only
when the desire has been satisfied or the person
is willing to trust his desire to the Great Law for
fulfillment can he be released, for he is *bound by
his thought and desire* and often follows it for hundreds of years, its very force making a wall around
him which shuts him away from the higher forces
which would otherwise help him to progress out of
his condition, as the average person would naturally do. In fact, the Soul remains in each Realm
until it learns the lessons of that Realm, realizes
wherein it made the mistakes which retarded its
growth and unfoldment, and evolves to the point
where it is ready to pass on to higher Realms. The
earth-bound entities are usually so dense and have
so much of earthly conditions attached to them
that under certain atmospheric conditions they
can appear to the objective sight of mortals—
and especially to animals, horses shying at these
so-called ghosts in the road, dogs bristling or cringing and whining at them, etc.—as a more or less

dense, cold, clammy cloud or ghost. It is well known that the proximity of a wraith or ghost brings to mortals a chill and perhaps a shiver of horror. The reason for this is that the dense astral body is so laden with water vapor that it is like a cold dense fog which abstracts heat from the living body it approaches, and this sudden loss of heat, like a cold damp wind, causes the chill. The sense of horror is due to the fact that most of such ghosts passed out under horrible conditions, which horror is communicated to the mortal contacted, although fear of the dead is also a contributing factor.

The love of parents which makes them remain close to the children left behind or the love of husband, wife or son for the one left on earth, while it keeps them in close touch with the dear ones, does not hold them in the sense in which the term is generally used, for in such cases they usually progress into the higher realms and in time learn to overshadow the loved ones mentally rather than in their astral bodies, and learn to communicate through telepathy.

Just as the dense physical body is left behind when the Soul leaves the realms of physical activity, so is the dense astral body left behind when the Soul dies to the lower realms of the astral. Here, just as there are graveyards for the discarded physical bodies on earth, so are there regions in the Realm of Reflection where the discarded and disintegrating astral bodies are gathered. But in that Realm where all is exposed to view, the disintegrating bodies cannot be covered up and have flowers and trees planted over them as on earth. Hence pupils who are still on earth sometimes wander into such regions when out in the astral just as they might wander into a physical graveyard, and are often badly frightened by the ghastly sights encountered, but a strong thought will immediately carry them up through or away from such regions.

Here again we find an analogous condition to earth, for just as many advanced Souls are teaching on earth the advisability of cremation, so in the astral Realms. Many who are following the higher teachings, invoke the higher potencies of fire and destroy these astral corpses as it were with a breath. This is an important work, for as we have explained many times, a low class of elementals sometimes takes possession of these discarded forms and masquerades as the person, thus deceiving many.

When the astral body is cast off, since it is finer and more enduring, it disintegrates much more slowly than the physical body. And under certain circumstances such a discarded astral body or empty shell can be temporarily inhabited by a mischievous or perhaps an evil elemental and so be galvanized into a semblance of the departed one. The memory-pictures still remaining in the astral brain can be stimulated and so the shell may apparently be made to remember names, places, incidents, etc., through which its former tenant had passed.

Such animated shells are not infrequently presented at seances and strive to be accepted as a genuine return of the deceased. But such fraud is easily detected and exposed by a challenge or by a determined and insistent desire that nothing shall manifest that is not what it purports to be. In such cases your intuition will warn you that something is wrong and will remind you to challenge the manifestation.

It is in this Realm of Reflection that the governing consciousness of plants, also ants, spiders and similar insects, resides. It is also as high as the consciousness of many trance mediums, and also the idiot ascends; for the idiot is often not merely defective, but is simply an human animal in which no human Soul has incarnated, hence is capable of developing only as an animal.

CHAPTER VIII

THE ETHEREAL REALM

"I am gone before your face
A moment's worth, a little space.
When ye come where I have stepped
Ye will wonder why ye wept."

After Death in Arabia, Arnold.

"For people having any acquaintance with
scientific history to shut their eyes to fact *when
definitely announced*, and to forbid investigation
or report concerning them on pain of ostracism—
is to imitate a bygone theological attitude in a
spirit of unintended flattery—a flattery which
from every point of view is eccentric."

Raymond, Lodge, 314.

THE Ethereal Realm is the Realm into which
the astral body rises after it has gotten rid of the
densest earth magnetism and the strongest of the
earth attractions; in other words, after the person
has given up the idea that it is necessary to stay near
the earth in order to exist or remain in touch with
his loved ones, or that he must still try to influence
and control the administration of the affairs he left
behind in the Physical World.

This Realm is the abode of the majority of intelli-

gent persons who have been away from the Physical
World long enough to learn the lessons of the lower
Realm of Reflection and who are gaining greater
freedom from earthly ties and reaching up for a
still higher and more spiritual life or who, as often
happens, learned many of the lessons of the Realm
of Reflection while still on earth, hence passed
rapidly through the lower Realms after leaving
the physical. This Realm is what was formerly
called the "summer land" by the spiritualists of
last century. Here there are branches of the great
schools of learning which are situated in the higher
Realms, established here for the training of those
in this Realm who desire to progress and wish
to understand the laws and conditions by which
their new life is governed. But the majority of the
inhabitants of this Realm continue for the most part
to pursue activities similar to those which occupied
their attention while in the Realm of Reflection, but
in a way more suited to their changed conditions.

From this Realm, as well as from the lower Realm
of Reflection, the departed ones can return and assume physical control of a subjective medium and
temporarily incarnate in the medium's body and use
it as they please, but in so doing they not only invariably bring back with them and reproduce in the
medium the same physical conditions with which
they passed out, but they also throw these conditions of suffering, grief, etc., over the loved ones
or any sensitive whom they approach; that is, until

they have been taught to communicate not through the subjective control but through the normal and *independent method* which will be described later on.[1] It should therefore be understood as a fundamental law of the Astral World that without special training no person in the astral can come close enough to contact the aura of his friends on earth without unconsciously and automatically bringing with him and imposing on the earthly friend the physical, astral and mental conditions which he suffered from or experienced as he left the body at death.

This explains why many sensitive persons soon develop the symptoms of the malady with which a deceased loved one passed out. Such persons suffer just as acutely as though they really had such a physical disease, yet a careful physical examination reveals all the vital organs in a normal condition. These are often diagnosed as imagination or "neurosis" or even "hysteria" and insanity by physicians who are not familiar with the results of psychic research or the laws of occultism. Such patients are simply suffering from the *astral conditions* unwittingly thrown over them by the deceased loved one who is trying to make them recognize him; and the stronger the tie was between them the greater the influence and consequent suffering. This frequently ceases or is "cured" when they recognize its source. If it is not it should be stopped by

---

[1] See page 225.

repeatedly challenging the departed one and demanding that he withdraw from their aura and remain outside it in the future; for such psychic conditions if long continued may act reflexly and set up the actual disease in its physical form. These are the stubborn cases which have "been given up by all doctors," yet are so frequently cured by Christian Science, affirmations, etc., the study, instruction and personal magnetism of the healer and the resulting discussions, making the departed one more or less aware of his responsibility for the conditions and inducing him to withdraw.

Such reflex psychic effects are strongest in the case of those who passed out through accident, in war or with acute and short illnesses. But above all they are strongest in the case of the suicide. Since all such persons have not lived out their normal physical life-period nor been prepared for life in the Astral World by a gradual loosening of the bonds of the flesh, they pass out full of physical magnetism, life-force and desire for a continued life in the Physical World, hence have a stronger and more physical force to throw over those left behind. In the former cases the deceased will be met by friends and loved ones on the other side and be taught how best to gain the desired recognition or how best to get along without it, while in the latter they are suddenly projected into the astral unannounced and unexpected and must learn to shift for themselves.

With the densest of earth conditions, thoughts and magnetism eliminated from their astral bodies, the inhabitants of this Realm are no longer such accurate duplicates of their earthly bodies and personalities. While it is possible for those who pass on in childhood or in full vigor of youth, manhood or womanhood, to reincarnate quickly from this Realm without passing on into the higher Realms and higher Worlds to complete their cycle of manifestation, it is by no means common.[2] Those who do reincarnate without entering the higher Realms are less well equipped for their new earth life, just as a child who leaves school before his education is completed is more or less handicapped by his lack of advanced training.

Those who do continue onward in their normal cycle through the Realms continue to grow and develop. Never do they grow old, however, but reach a full Soul maturity, and are clothed in a form which expresses the point of evolution and development which their Soul had attained, and remain at that point. Hence there are child Souls who appear as beautiful children and there are mature Souls whose age is shown only by the look of Wisdom, altho they may have left the Physical World in childhood.

Those who do, under special conditions, reincarnate immediately merely live out the unexpired term of their former life-period. Hence the new life often ends abruptly. On the other hand those who pass on during old age or after a depleting illness grow younger until the period of the most

---

[2] Except after great wars and cataclysms, after which some thus incarnate to finish out the balance of their life-cycle—sometimes through the same mother—thus abnormally cut short by the war, etc. But only comparatively few do this.

perfect state of vigorous maturity or the point of
their Soul development is reached. And they remain
in this perfected state until they leave behind them
the dense astral body and pass on into the higher
Realms. Never is there old age in this or higher
Realms.

Both of the above classes, however, as they return to commune with their friends on earth find it
necessary to assume at first the exact appearance by
which they were known on earth, lest their friends
fail to recognize them in their changed appearance.
For instance, a Soul passing on as an infant would
always present itself at first as an infant, although in
reality it may have attained maturity, while an aged
person would present himself with all the marks of
age and feebleness, although in reality restored to
the full vigor of maturity.

The inhabitants of this Realm can see the physical conditions of their mortal friends only when
those friends are thinking about them and sending
them their magnetism or when the necessary earthly
magnetism is furnished by a medium. In all cases
communication is easier if the mortals send the departed ones love and sympathy, also if they know
something of life after death. Those still in the flesh
can therefore be of the greatest help to their loved
ones who have passed on, by studying the laws of
the higher Realms—not merely dabbling in phenomena—and by familiarizing themselves with the
spiritual truths and philosophy such as is promul-

gated by the Order of Christian Mystics. For if a mental call is sent to the loved ones, they will come and study with the mortal and thus rapidly learn the true explanation of the many puzzling problems which confront them in the higher life. Also they can more readily grasp the truth of the teachings and see deeper into their meaning, and in return they can make it easier for the mortal loved one to grasp them. Definite periods for study together can thus be made and such appointments are scrupulously kept by those in the Astral World. It is as impolite for the mortal not to keep an appointment made with an astral friend as it would be to break an engagement with a physical friend.

While those in the astral are, as it were, a step above those in the Physical World and can see many events and conditions somewhat before they manifest on earth—just as a person standing on a platform can see over the heads of the crowd and tell them what is approaching—no matter how sincere they may be, they can seldom predict accurately the time of physical manifestation for that which they see. This is because there are so many currents of force, either earthly or karmic, which may intervene between that which seems destined and the time of its physical manifestation, that may either hasten or retard the event. Again there is no time as earth measures it in those Realms, for time there is marked by experience or rather sensation. Therefore, if a mortal felt a very strong desire for an event to come, which was plainly seen by an excarnate one, it would be described as coming quickly or even to be here, according to the strong sensation of desire sent out by the mortal, or if it were dreaded the excarnate one might see it as far off.

While the thing we dread is really drawn to us, yet in this World of Sensation, especially in this Etheric Realm, the greatest sensation is that of love. So when inhabitants of this Realm come to loved ones on earth they are so filled with love for the mortal that, not yet having attained all wisdom, their greatest desire is to comfort them. Hence the thing the loved one longs for is seen quite plainly by the excarnate one and appears very close, while the thing dreaded is pushed back out of vision. This partly accounts for the many serious mistakes made in messages received from the Astral World, the others being due to ignorance or to malice and often intentional and elaborate deception.[3]

In this Realm the clothing is somewhat different

---

[3] For example, "A young American named Dean Bridgemen Conner went to Mexico City in 1894, was employed as electrician in a theatre, became ill with typhoid fever, and in March, 1895, was reported by the Consul to have died at the American Hospital, and to have been buried in the American cemetery. Some months afterward, however, the young man's father had a dream in which his son appeared and informed him that he was alive and in captivity, being held for ransom in Mexico. Mrs. Piper was consulted by friends of the Conners, trance sittings were held, and the controls. . . . purported to trace his movement, and whereabouts. They confirmed the father's dream, and stated that the missing man was in or near Pueblo,

from that commonly used in the Realm of Reflection, for while many persons wear for some time, even years, costumes similar to those they had been in the habit of wearing on earth, later on most of those belonging to Christian nations don white robes. This is largely the result of the orthodox thoughts held for so many years while on earth, namely, that a white robe is the proper costume for life after death. Hence they are clad in it as naturally as a tree is clad with leaves. Also white represents purity, and since it is in the Ethereal Realm that many of the higher ideals and desires held while on earth are experienced and worked out, those who have learned to value purity are trying to express it in this way.

In this Realm there are many of the old philosophers and men of Science who have made for themselves what might be called a little heaven of their own, in which they surround themselves with the thought forces they themselves created when on earth, and these are continually strengthened by the thought forces of all similarly minded persons on earth. Sometimes such an one lives in this mental isolation for centuries, just as they did for years on earth.

---

in a building which they described, guarded by a man whom they described and named. Several investigators went to Mexico, one after the other, and it was finally established by Mr. Philpot, who found the nurse who was with Conner when he died, that the Consul's report was perfectly true, and that the dream and the trance 'information' were, so far as Conner was concerned, entirely wrong." *Psychical Investigations*, Hill, 222.

Again there are those Philanthropists who have built up some Utopian ideal for the betterment of humanity, perhaps have sought to found a colony which has failed on earth. Here they do found the colony and live in it, until the defects which made it fail on earth become so apparent to the founder that he learns his lesson from them. Then the colony likewise is dissolved, all that is good being withdrawn. The mistake lives only as a soul memory, and will be avoided in the next earth life.

There are those in this Realm who are laboriously following modes of life which they had built up while on earth as representing their ideal of attainment. Here we find churches of all denominations filled with devout worshipers listening to sermons on their favorite subjects. Here we find monasteries in which devout priests live lives of extreme simplicity and abstemiousness, spending long hours in prayer and fasting and following most conscientiously the highest ideals of the monastic life, as they had always longed to but had never been able to fully express on earth. Here also are societies of devout nuns, sisters of charity, etc., as well as splendid centers for almost every religion, in which all those things the devotees longed for on earth yet never attained are experienced.

Here also are model homes, model farms, settlements, tenements, cities, and every dream of the philanthropist apparently fulfilled. For this Realm is where dreams seem to come true, or put it more truthfully, this is the Realm in which all the religious and

Utopian dreams attempted on earth must be experienced to the fullest degree conceived on earth, until the force which put them forth has been exhausted and it is realized that they are still imperfect. This will be only when the Soul has found that it still longs for something greater; that all these perfected material things so longed for on earth still fall far short of perfect bliss. They are enjoyed here for a time just as a child will continue to amuse itself with certain toys until it outgrows them. Ultimately the Soul also outgrows these earthly toys, sooner or later according to how much true unselfishness, true humanitarianism and love is contained in them. But gradually the Soul learns through experience just where all these things fall short, hence is ready to see something higher, at which time it dies to this Realm and passes on to the higher Realms.

Many wear robes of red, yellow, blue or other colors, some light and beautiful, others dark and somber, according to their own inner spiritual qualifications. As we have said in a previous chapter, in the lower Realms the emanations from physical things are built into the corresponding astral creations, but as the higher Realms are reached the denser emanations fade out or are left behind, the clothing being built out of the characteristic substance of each Realm of each World.

This is the Realm reached in light sleep; during the administration of anesthetics, during certain forms of trance, and in mild delirium.

CHAPTER IX

THE VITAL REALM OR REALM OF FORMATION

"Behold the Hosts of Souls. Watch how they hover o'er the stormy sea of human life, and how, exhausted, bleeding, broken-winged, they drop one after the other on the swelling waves. Tossed by fierce winds, chased by the gale, they drift into the eddies and disappear within the first great vortex."

The Voice of the Silence, Blavatsky, 9.

THE Realm of the life-force or the Vital Realm is the one in which the life-force is taking on forms and animating them. It is the Realm into which the ideals, thought-forms or patterns of all things destined to manifest on earth descend in materialization. That is to say, all that is projected outward as an ideal or idea from the Divine Mind, as well as all that is created by the mind of man, must in the course of its descending arc take on more and more materialized stages of embodiment until its form finally reaches a physical expression. It is in this Vital Realm that the various currents of the life-force flow into and through the pattern or thought-form of the thing to be manifested, carrying with them the ethereal astral matter and building it into the thought-pattern until the thought-pattern takes on the limitations of matter and becomes an objective astral form, ready to descend one step further into the still denser and still more limited Physical World. The astral model thus formed, in its turn has the inherent tendency to absorb or build matter into itself, and the water vapor in it tends to disintegrate or dissolve physical forms not held coherent by the life-force, as rain dissolves a clod. Hence the forms described in the previous chapter as being created in the Etheric Realm are ultimately dissolved and disintegrated, for, being but the building of astral etheric matter into the ideals or thought-forms created during earth life, when the vital life-force or Spiritual reality is poured into them they are like summer mists dissolved by the sun.

It is in this Realm that the ideal pattern of the bodily form desired by the Soul seeking incarnation descends and takes on an astral form or body. It is probably some phase of this Realm which Maeterlinck sensed and so beautifully described in *The Blue Bird*, where the Souls of many children are represented as hovering over the earth seeking incarnation. There is, however, a difference between Maeterlinck's poetical vision and the reality. For while what seem to be hosts of Souls wait in this Realm for an opportunity to incarnate without leaving the astral and passing on into the higher Worlds of Bliss—rushing downward at every opening of the

door into incarnation, literally surrounding
every expectant mother, the less developed ones
fighting for a chance to take possession, the
struggle often producing those sudden changes of
character, outbreaks of hysteria, etc., exhibited by
many mothers during the first few months of the
puerperium—yet the great majority of Souls do not
incarnate in this way. The majority, after passing
through the various Realms of the Astral World pass
on into the Higher Worlds where they are united
to their Father-in-Heaven, their Progenitor. These
Souls on returning to incarnation descend into a
special division of the Astral World called the Hall
of Lethe, where they are specially prepared to take
the step earthward. Among these are the advanced
ones who have chosen to incarnate to accomplish
a certain mission, and who have likewise chosen
their parents and their environments. These, after
their descent from the Higher Worlds, wait in what
might be compared to an ante-room during a period
in which they deliberately make preparation, the
first step of which is to wean themselves from
the memory of the life of bliss in which they
have reveled during their existence in the Higher
Worlds. During this period they gradually fall
into a sort of dreaming sleep in which they forget
the life just completed and instead are filled with
dreams of great compassion for humanity, great
desire to enter earth life to help and comfort or
to fill some great mission left incomplete in
past lives, or sometimes with only great love

and eagerness to come into touch with a certain
mother or family. Such preparation is necessary to
advanced Souls, for without it the memory of their
heaven home would make earth life intolerable
to them. Many undeveloped ones simply swarm
earthward, drawn by the great attraction of
sensation and either entirely ignorant or unmindful
of anything else. They have gone no further than
the Etheric Realm, hence are driven into incarnation
again by desire for more earthly experiences that
they may have more sensation.

   This Realm may therefore be called the "dark-
room" or "cabinet" of the earth, for it serves the
same purpose as does the cabinet of the materializing medium. All materialization follows the same
law, but in this case it is the natural and inevitable
materialization of that which is on the positive
or *downward arc* descending into manifestation,
while the materialization which takes place in a
séance room is an *artificial attempt* to bring back
into physical manifestation those who are on the
upward arc of evolution. Since in this practice all
the normal currents are reversed, such an attempt
must necessarily be *abnormal and degenerating*.
We do not question the phenomena produced at
materializations, but we deplore the *method* generally employed.

   In this Realm there are two distinct currents of
force, one which is gathering the creative forces
from the higher spiritual Realms—the vital life-
force which is ever flowing downward through the

lower Astral Realms, and is eternally bringing into formation the true spiritual conceptions of those things which are to manifest on earth—and an upward current which is unfolding and then disintegrating and transmuting all other forms, just as we have said that the ideals of the Etheric Realm are gradually dissolved. We might roughly compare this Realm to the retort of an alchemist into which the base metals are placed while the flames lick up the gases, melt the metals, and ultimately produce new substance (gold).

When students occasionally succeed in penetrating into the *upper* strata of this Realm, they enter a condition of intense darkness in which swirling and often terrifying currents of force like winds are encountered which seem almost to tear them to pieces. These currents produce vortices of force which gyrate with various rates of speed, and since they are continually sucking astral matter into patterns or moulds, they would tend to disintegrate the astral body of one who lingered too long in close proximity to them. This is often confused with the "outer darkness"[1] so often referred to in various scriptures, in which state there is "weeping and wailing and gnashing of teeth," for the various currents vibrate, purr and sing or wail and howl like so many demons. Here is also heard the wail of the soulless entities whose bodies are being disintegrated.

---

[1] See page 146.

Under certain conditions these currents are strong enough to sweep the astral body of a mortal out of its path of evolution or even out of incarnation, or they could sweep the astral body of a deceased mortal away from its astral companions and all earthly ties. Therefore a student should never seek to penetrate the upper strata of this Vital Realm without a good reason for so doing and without the guidance of One Who Knows and is able to protect him. Again, this current of blackness is the River Acheron which the Soul must cross to reach the higher Realms.[2] Hence the prayers to be found in all religions for the safe passage and protection of the departed.

While the upper strata of this third Realm are intensely and almost palpably dark and black, its lower strata are intensely vivid and scintillating with a brilliant play of color, full of the most gorgeous flowers, ravishing melodies and intoxicating perfumes. One whose consciousness vibrates to the lower strata of this Realm would seem to be in a mighty kaleidoscope of ever-changing forms, some rising like cloud pictures only to be dissipated, others swirling round or floating aimlessly, yet momentarily taking on new forms. The colors, sounds, perfumes, etc., exist here *en masse* awaiting embodiment in the various forms to which they are affinitized, much the same as masses of color are poured out on an

---

[2] See Chapter II.

artist's palette awaiting their embodiment in the picture. Beside the Souls waiting for incarnation, the inhabitants of this Realm are swift flying Angelic Beings, and the higher classes of elementals, which will be treated of in another chapter.

Here also the thought-forms of all the inventions, scientific conceptions and philanthropic plans, etc. which have been conceived in the Mental Realm of the Astral World—as a result of the mind of some mortal responding to the ideal of that thing which exists in the Mental World far above the astral—descend to be embodied in astral matter. These astral models do not remain in this Realm, however, but are swept down into the Etheric Realm by the great downpouring Currents of Manifestation. There they remain until some one can give them some form of physical expression. If they are abandoned and not given physical expression, as soon as the creative mental force which conceived them is exhausted they again ascend into the Vital Realm where their form is disintegrated and as much of the ideal as they embodied is released to return to its source in the Mental World. If they are not expressed yet are not abandoned by their conceiver, they remain in the Etheric Realm to greet him when he passes into the astral where he will continue to perfect them. Those which are perfected remain in a special stratum between the Vital and Etheric Realms as perfected models. Here in what might be called the Pattern Museum are the wonderful inventions of the ancient Atlanteans and others, including aeroplanes, etc., which reached great perfection because they were brought forth by the earlier races under the direct guidance of the Masters, as a child paints a perfect picture with the teacher guiding his hand. All these newly found patterns are phases of the manifestation of the ideals that have just come into concrete expression fresh from the "dark-room" above and before the seeds of Karma have begun to unfold and modify them.

The karmic seeds usually modify the perfect expression in the direction of imperfection and further limitation, because by the time astral form is reached, the ideal is embodied in a more or less crude state and its more ideal expression must be achieved through evolution in the Physical World. The mistakes of the past must be subtracted from the ideal, hence modify and limit the perfect pattern. For instance, the Soul desiring to incarnate builds up a perfect mental pattern of the kind of a body it desires to have on earth, and this pattern is embodied in astral matter in this Vital Realm. But as soon as this perfect model is fashioned there is automatically and magnetically attracted to it the Karma of the past life. This Karma may so greatly modify the perfect model that it may be born defective or even crippled or diseased. Such a modified model might be far from the one desired by the Soul, but would be the best it could create in view of the causes it had set up in a past life. This model would be further modified by the physical and mental heredity—also the facial and bodily appearance—of the family through which the incarnation took place.

CHAPTER X

THE DESIRE REALM

OBSESSING ENTITIES

"And there was in their synagogue a man with
an unclean spirit. . . . And Jesus rebuked him,
saying: 'Hold thy peace, and come out of him.'
And when the unclean spirit had torn him, and
cried out with a loud voice, he came out of him."

St. Mark, i, 23-5.

To make our study of the Astral World complete
it is necessary for us to discuss a most unpleasant Realm, but since it is largely the influences
from this Realm which give to the astral its terrors
and which bring to humanity its greatest horrors
and suffering, it is most important that a thorough
understanding of the conditions, and a practical
method of how to master the influences, be spread
abroad as widely as possible among students of the
occult and those who are investigating conditions
of life after death.

Just as the Fourth globe of the Earth Chain[1] — our
physical planet — is the lowest point in the down-

---

[1] See *The Voice of Isis*, Curtiss, 204.

ward arc of descent of Spirit into material
manifestation, and hence contains the densest
form of matter in which the Spirit must learn to
express itself, so the fourth Realm of the Astral
World is the lowest state in which the consciousness
of the departed manifests. The physical body is
not the lowest in the sense of the least spiritual
vehicle through which the consciousness of man
is expressed. It is but the outer shell[2] through
which both the animal soul and the Spiritual
Soul or Divine Self (Atma, Buddhi and Higher
Manas) must manifest in the Physical World. In
theosophical terms the animal soul creates the body
of desire (*Kama Rupa*), while the Spiritual Soul
creates the soul body or *Buddhic Rupa*, both of
which find earthly expression through the physical
body. The great aim of evolution is to make the
personality the earthly expression of the Spiritual
Soul or Higher Self to the same degree that it now
expresses the animal soul. For it is the Spiritual
Soul which is made in the image of God, while alas
it is the image of the animal soul only which man
too often imprints upon his body.

The astral bodies, therefore, of those dwelling
in this Realm are lower, denser, more material and
impure than the bodies of those dwelling in any other
Realm of the Astral World. This Realm in many
of its aspects overlaps the Realm of Reflection,
but while both are dense, close to earth and ruled
by earthly desires, the Desire Realm contains the

---

[2] Not created, like the spiritual man of *Genesis*, i, 27, but "formed" or evolved
"out of the dust of the ground" for the use of the Divine Self, as *Genesis*, ii,
7, tells us.

grossest, most impure and degraded desires, the persons having sordid, earthly, but not necessarily impure or evil desires occupying the border-land between the two Realms. This, therefore, is the Realm in which we find those who while on earth were murderers, habitual or periodic drunkards, criminals, procurers, profligates, prostitutes, degenerates, drug fiends, etc., together with those who secretly desired to give free rein to their passions and appetites, but who were restrained, not by a desire to be good and pure, but merely because their social, business or political position made it good policy. In this Realm, unhampered by any such considerations, they would find an opportunity for unbridled license and unlimited gratification of all their evil tendencies, provided they could find the necessary means for their expression.

A knowledge of the conditions obtaining in this Realm of the Astral World offers a powerful argument against capital punishment; for the execution of a murderer or other criminal merely removes his hampering physical body, which at least limited his evil activities to the Physical World. Executing or destroying the physical body sets him free in the Astral World, embittered against society because of the experiences he has passed through, his heart filled with hatred and revenge, and able to throw his force over any mind which is open to such thoughts. He therefore seeks to wreak his vengeance upon society and gratify his desires by controlling and obsessing as many sensitive persons as possible;

those whose auras are sufficiently open to
his influence to permit his entrance into their
consciousness. For instance, a sensitive once picked
up and handled an axe in a museum and at once
came into rapport with the ancient savage who
had fashioned and used it. With such contact came
the almost overwhelming desire to experience the
sensation of delight felt by the savage as his axe
crushed through the skull of his enemy.

But unless sensitives harbor some thought
or trait corresponding to that of the astral entity,
which forms a line of affinity over which he can
enter their auras, he cannot control them. Once an
opening is made, an entrance gained and his influence or control established, he gradually forces
his victim to carry out his ideas of revenge, taking
as many lives as possible to pay up for society's
having taken his life. Thus, while in the physical body he could commit but comparatively few
crimes, when set free in the Astral World he can
influence dozens or hundreds to commit similar
crimes. Murders committed under such obsessions
are those concerning which the mortal executing the crime either remembers nothing about or
can give no reason for, except that he acted under an "irresistible impulse" or perhaps says that
"God" or a "Voice" told and impelled him to do the
deed. Such cases are usually pronounced insane.
These are crimes committed under some form of
mania, paranoia, etc. While medical science says
that such a person is not responsible for his acts,

occult science says that *he is:* for he is responsible for opening his mind to such thoughts as will permit the entrance of the obsessing entity; he is responsible for every act, word and deed committed by him, whether willed by him or not, and must pay the karmic penalty. It is true that many who become criminals under such conditions are not inherently criminal nor viciously wicked, but are simply sensitives whose astral centers have been more or less broken down and whose weak wills, negative mental states, and lack of spiritual development makes them an easy prey to obsession. But even for this condition they are strictly responsible, for ignorance of the law is no excuse for its violation.

Remember, therefore, that harboring thoughts of anger, hatred, revenge or any form of "getting even" with some one whom you feel has wronged you, opens your aura to those in the Astral World who harbour similar thoughts and who will strive to enter your consciousness over the avenue thus opened and stir up and *augment* your hatred and urge you to execute a far more terrible form of "getting even" than you would entertain or even think of by yourself. The practice of forgiving others is therefore enjoined on all occult and spiritual students, for as long as you hold antagonism toward any one *you bind yourself to that one* with a powerful tie and also open yourself to obsessing forces along that line.

The drunkards who have left the Physical World also form a large and important class in the Desire

Realm, for they, too, seek to gratify their desires through sensitive mortals. In fact, our long experience with cases of this kind leads us to the conclusion that nearly every case of confirmed and habitual or periodic drunkenness is the result of an obsession.

That medical science is already beginning to suspect this truth is shown in an article by Dr. T. D. Crothers connected with "a research foundation organized in Hartford, Conn., to take up this new question, and seek an explanation of the puzzling phenomena of the drink evil and the paradoxical symptoms of the victims." This eminent authority tells us, in *The Medical Record* of January 6, 1917, that: "The laboratories have pointed out the specific action of alcohol on the cells and tissues, and their conclusions have literally revolutionized the theories of the past and opened up a new world, that is only partially discovered. Beyond this, there is another Realm and new country of causes of physiological and *psychological forces* that are practically unknown. . . . This work starts from the conviction that there are distinct physical and *psychical causes* preceding the use of alcohol, governing its rise and fall with the certainty of any other phenomena of nature. As examples: What are the causes of periodical drinking? Why do large numbers of most excellent men *suddenly* use spirits to great excess for a few days or weeks, then stop and resume their normal condition of healthy temperate living? These unexplainable so-called *nerve storms* occur at either regular or irregular periods. In some instances the regularity is pronounced and can be predicted regardless of the efforts of the person to avert it. The free interval between these drink storms is marked by most exemplary living and conduct, and the drink periods are equally prominent in insane and idiotic acts. Persons of this class are seen in all circles of society and very often among the most intellectual brain workers who are respected and are men of affairs. . . . Other instances are of men after a half a lifetime of sobriety, temperate work and living, suddenly become users of spirits; in addition resisting all efforts to correct, and finally culminating in pauperism and death. There is no explanation of the causes which impel men to drink continuously down to death. This begins sometimes at the height of prosperity and achievement or following disaster to property and family. . . . Young men in college, brought up under the same conditions and influences, bring out this fact. Without any special causes or reasons one uses spirits to excess and becomes a cripple and dies early. . . .

"What condition of the brain and nervous system predisposes to and favors the outbreak of a craze for narcotism from spirits is unknown. Apparently they were elation from success and triumphs or despair from loss and disappointment, but evidently there are *some other conditions beyond these* to account for the trouble. To the casual observer all these are traceable to the one cause—alcohol; but when

tested carefully, *this fails*. The exceptions are so
numerous and complex as to indicate beyond
question other causes and forces. In reality the
phenomena and symptomatology are only effects,
dating from *other causes further* back."

There is but one explanation that covers *all the
facts* and phenomena, and that is the one here presented. To explain how this condition is brought
about we cannot do better than to quote from what
we have already said in *The Voice of Isis:*[3]

"The human body is the Temple of the Living
God. Within it are certain vital centers comparable
to doors[4] which open into inner shrines. Using
these centers as points of contact, the life forces
from the higher planes flow into the physical body
through them as an electrical current flows through
a wire. . . . These centers or doors are normally
protected by nature with oily coverings or sheaths
(composed of both astral and physical matter) which
permit the flow of the normal life-forces and protect
them from all others. These doors should be opened
only by a gradual purification and development of
the protecting sheaths. Normally this takes place
as a natural growth resulting from a life of mental
and bodily purity, and intense spiritual aspiration.
It should not be a forced or hothouse growth, for

---

[3] Pages 98-104.
[4] In ancient times a door meant a passage way leading into a chamber and was
not used as commonly as now to mean that which closed the passage way.

each door must be opened and dosed under the absolute control of the will. . . . Once these sheaths are destroyed, the person is no longer able to close the doors and so becomes an easy prey to the denizens of the astral. Such an one becomes a helpless victim to *any* and *all* sorts of psychic imposition and deception. . . . There are several abnormal ways in which the oily protecting sheaths can be broken down and the doors thrown open, chief among which are the use of alcohol and narcotic drugs. Chemically speaking, ordinary alcohol is ethyl-hydroxide. The ethyl (the spirit) vibrates to the highest rate reached by mere physical matter, the point where matter transcends the physical and enters the astral, the ethyl actually functioning on both planes. Narcotic drugs also contain an ethyl element. The ethyl when taken into the body immediately seeks to escape into the astral, and it naturally follows the usual avenues of communication between the two planes. But in escaping it passes through the centers in a reverse direction to the normal currents and gradually burns off the insulating sheaths until in time they are utterly destroyed, just as an electrical insulation might be burned off by interference with the normal flow of the current.

"This breakdown may be very rapid, as in the case of an habitual drunkard or a drug fiend, or it may be insidious and not show markedly for several incarnations, but the result is certain and every indulgence in the substances mentioned is a step

toward the end. Ultimately this leaves the doors
unguarded and open for all the horrors of the lowest
Astral Realm to rush in and take possession of
the 'Temple of the Living God' thus desecrated.
Bulwer-Lytton gives a realistic description of some
of these horrors in his occult novel, *Zanoni*. In that
story the student opened the doors abnormally by
the use of drugs, and being unable to close them
through fright at the sights that met his gaze, was
haunted until his death. . . . It is our duty to
give our sympathy and help to this class of sorely
afflicted ones, for since it took many lives to
break down the protective sheaths, it will require
a long hard fight to rebuild them. Hence do not
let such unfortunate ones become discouraged. No
matter how many times they may fall back into
the old habits, every effort to conquer aids in the
rebuilding. And the very fierceness of the struggle
will ultimately strengthen the Soul. . . . These
sheaths are not broken down in one incarnation,
but since in each incarnation there is a tendency
to repeat the same old mistakes until they are
conquered, so in each incarnation there is a
tendency to increase the weakness brought over
from the past until the final break-down comes. The
rebuilding must necessarily follow the same law,
i.e., be brought about by gradual accomplishment
through determined and persistent constructive
effort."

Our teachings on this subject have been strikingly
corroborated since their first publication in 1912 by

Judge Hatch in 1914 through Elsa Barker's *Letters from a Living Dead Man*,[5] as follows:

"Desiring one day to see the particular kind of hell to which a drunkard would be likely to go I put myself in a sympathetic and neutral state, so that I could see into both Realms. . . . A young man with restless eyes and a troubled face entered one of these 'gin palaces'. . . . He was leaning on the bar drinking. . . . And close to him, taller than he and bending over him, with its repulsive, bloated, ghastly face pressed close to his was one of the most horrible astral beings which I have ever seen. . . . It was literally sucking the liquor-soaked life of its victim, absorbing him, using him in the successful attempt to enjoy vicariously the passion which death had intensified. The young man who leaned on the bar in that gilded palace of gin was filled with a nameless horror and sought to leave the place; but the arms of the thing that was now his master clutched him tighter and tighter, the sodden, vaporous cheek was pressed close to his, the desire of the vampire creature aroused an answering desire in its victim, and the young man demanded another glass."

Even a moderate drinker gradually breaks down his doors until finally he reaches a point where, without definite training, he can no longer protect his aura from invasion by those who affinitize with

---

[5] Pages 173-4.

him in a desire for alcoholic stimulation. As such obsessing entities gain more control over the victim, they urge him to greater and greater excesses. The victim's innate goodness, respectability and spiritual guidance usually make him rebel at first and he is filled with shame, remorse and sincere repentance, the force of which may be strong enough to enable him to resist perhaps for months. Then his *unconquered self-indulgence* and fancied security, his fancied ability to "take a drink or let it alone" leads him again to open the door, and again the obsession takes place.

A few instances which have come under our personal observation may serve as concrete illustrations of the disastrous results of this form of obsession. A brilliant young newspaper man in a large Eastern city was an occasional user of the lighter drinks, the so-called "social glass" of beer and wine, but did not care for and could not stand whiskey, brandy, gin, etc. He had an older brother, however, who died suddenly after a prolonged spree. The younger man was of the quick, impressionable, sensitive artistic temperament and somewhat psychic. Soon after his brother's death he complained to us that his brother was coming to him psychically and urging him to drink. Whenever he wanted merely a glass of beer, the brother would throw over him a fierce desire for brandy. Little by little he gradually yielded to this augmented desire, until he finally realized where it was leading him and began to resist. He then related to us the terrible battles, lasting sometimes for hours and days he was having to prevent the brother from completely obsessing him. At last, tired out with the struggle, he would give in "for this once," as he would promise himself. Then he would start in drinking brandy, whiskey, gin, etc., which by this time he had come to loathe. His stomach was so sensitive and rebelled against it so strongly at first that he would often have to drink the third or fourth glass of whiskey or brandy before his stomach would retain it. But the will of the obsessing brother was so strong that the younger was forced to persist until the liquor could be retained, and then continue until the debauch had lasted from several days to a week or two. When he was utterly exhausted and his life-force completely sapped, the brother would leave him for a few weeks until he recovered. Then would come another awful struggle to resist going on another spree.

Another most remarkable case of successive obsession was brought to our attention in Chicago. Mr. X. was ordinarily a man of much firmness, determination and strength of will, and while a moderate drinker, had never allowed liquor to overcome him until some four years ago, when he had a long spree. He soon got himself under control again and solemnly promised himself and wife that he would never thenceforth allow himself to become enslaved by his desire for drink. However, he still continued to drink moderately. He was a house painter and was closely associated with three other painters employed by the same firm, all of the other three being hard drinkers. Three years ago one of these three died from alcoholism, and a year later, almost on the same day, another died. Last January, the third and last of the three, after a long debauch, committed suicide on the anniversary of the second one's death. This last man was the foreman of the gang in which Mr. X. and the others worked, and had devoted all his spare time to drink and the pursuit of women. Mr. X. had been a close friend of his and upon his death was appointed to his position as foreman. Now the direct evidence of the obsession of Mr. X. begins with the death of his friend, the foreman, last January. Mrs. X. states that since that time her husband seems utterly unable to control his desire for liquor and has been getting steadily worse. He has experienced periods of great remorse, during which he would swear never to drink again, but would then go out and drink until his money was gone, being absent from home several days and leaving his family without money for a week at a time. During these sprees he would also visit the same class of women as did his dead foreman and former companion, although previous to this time he had never been a licentious man. Both Mr. X. and his wife are somewhat psychic, and both have seen the departed foreman enter their flat as a dark and chilling spectre, especially one night when they saw him come in from a narrow hall that

led to a room in which they knew a drunken man
was sleeping off his debauch.

Here we have a series of obsessions which gradually killed off one after the other of the original
group of four, until now only Mr. X. is left. Each
departed one naturally returned to the group with
which he had been so closely associated and *added
his craving* for drink to that of the ones left behind,
driving them to still further excesses. This accumulated force so overwhelmed the foreman that he was
driven to suicide to get rid of the obsessing demons,
and it bids fair to overwhelm his successor Mr. X.,
unless he takes most energetic steps to rid himself
of their influence.

An instance of an unsuccessful attack of a similar kind is the case of a student of this Order, this
time a woman, a psychic who had been trained
according to these teachings and who understood
how to maintain her self-control and protect herself. She was entering the elevator of a large office
building when she felt her feather neck-scarf
pulled from her neck. But the elevator door had
closed ere she could turn around, and she was
obliged to go on up to the office where her business errand called her. In the office, while standing
near a certain desk, a feeling of intense depression and horror came over her, which made her
fear that the man at the desk was contemplating
suicide. On descending to the street entrance she
asked the elevator starter if he had seen anything
of her neck-scarf. "Yes," he said, "I saw you drop

it. You will find it back there in the corner." As she walked back to the darker part of the hallway, a man presented himself to her psychic vision and accosted her. When she asked what he wanted, he said that it was he who caused her scarf to drop off in an effort to attract her attention, as he knew she could communicate with him and he wished her to do him a great favor. He told her that he formerly had the desk near which she had stood in the office she had visited, and a few months ago had committed suicide in his chair at the desk, following a prolonged spree. He said he had not had a drink since passing out, and as he was suffering intensely for one, he begged her to go and take a drink for him so he could get the stimulation of the alcohol by contact with her aura. He even offered to guide her to the "ladies entrance" of a certain high-class café of which he knew, where she could drink quite unobserved. This she, of course, refused to do, but said as she was thirsty herself she would go and get a glass of ice cream soda, if that would do him any good. He said he did not want a soda, and grew quite angry and abusive and tried to force her to enter the café as she passed by. She resisted, however, but told us that she had never so wanted a drink of whiskey in her life, in fact, never knew before what the craving was. When she bought her soda and tried to drink it, he threw his resentment and disgust over her so strongly that the very sight of the soda nauseated her and she had to leave it untouched. The fact of the suicide having been committed at the desk this lady visited was afterward verified by us.

The primary cause for giving way to drink in the beginning is *selfishness and self-indulgence*. Many moderate drinkers are the "good fellows" of the community because they have developed their affections and love-nature to a considerable degree, but without a corresponding gain in wisdom and self-control. Hence the very development of their love-nature tends to further self-indulgence. Many moderate drinkers are quite sensitive to the influence of the Astral World, even though they do not know it or recognize it as such. As they can find no other means of satisfying the inner craving for some form of stimulation—which is really a craving for the spiritual stimulus and thrill of satisfaction which comes only from vibrating in harmony with the spiritual ideals and guidance of the Higher Self, *the only real satisfaction in life*—they take to alcohol, since it gives them a temporary touch with the astral and a sort of ephemeral, pseudo-satisfaction, but with the inevitable reaction. Others drink in an effort to drown out the inner craving for true satisfaction which is more or less active in every heart; for the satisfaction which comes only from spiritual growth and attainment but which they either do not understand or refuse to admit and seek.

Remember, therefore, that permanently to cure drunkenness, so it will not recur, the tendency to

self-indulgence and irresponsibility for one's actions
must be boldly faced and determinedly overcome.
The immediate remedy, however, is to impress
upon the mind of the victim that the irresistible
craving which leads him to the excesses he is so
ashamed of, and which he so bitterly repents, is
not alone his own depraved desires, *but the desire
of a discarnate drunkard* who is seeking to satisfy
himself through obsessing the self-indulgent victim.
"Thought arises before desire. The thought acts on
the brain, the brain on the organ, and then the desire
awakens."[6] The following directions, quoted from
a letter written by the Teacher of the Order to such
a victim, and whose faithful following has entirely
cured him and many others, may prove helpful here.

"The real cause of your trouble is not with your
desire alone, but because you permit a discarnate
drinker to enter your aura and create within you
an excessive desire for liquor, that he may satisfy
his craving at the expense of your body and your
life-forces. If you will earnestly take yourself in
hand *and follow out our directions exactly*, you can
drive this influence away and free yourself from
the habit. Repeat to yourself again and again that
the desire for drink *is not your desire*, and that you
will not permit anyone to rule and ruin your life.
Dwell on this idea continually. Keep saying that
you will permit no drunkard thus to obsess and control you. Fix that idea firmly in mind. Repeat the

<hr>

[6] *The Secret Doctrine*, Blavatsky, iii, 573.

Morning Prayer[7] as soon as you awake every morning, and mentally see the Light of the Christ pouring down over you in a flood of pure, white light that shall penetrate every cell of your being and drive out every evil thing as light drives out darkness, and shall then surround you with a wall of living fire like the shell of an egg, into which no discarnate entity or evil thing can penetrate. Also repeat the *Prayer for Light*[8] and recall the vision again and again during the day, especially whenever you feel tempted.

"Also when you feel the old desire coming over you, say to yourself: 'In the name of the Living Christ *I demand* that you leave me and keep away. I will not yield *myself to you*, and I demand that you begone.' Talk just as earnestly and determinedly as though some old drunkard was before you in the flesh and trying to force you to drink with him. Do not get excited or have the least fear, but talk calmly and with absolute confidence in your power thus to protect yourself and conquer. No matter how hard he pleads, or what plausible arguments he may present—which may at first seem to be your own thoughts, but which will merely be his desire thrown upon your consciousness—as to why you should take 'just one more drink,' absolutely refuse, and keep saying: 'In the name of the Living Christ begone!' In the Astral World the Christ-force is a consuming fire, and if you sincerely and

---

[7] See Appendix.
[8] See Appendix.

earnestly invoke it with all your heart and
determination, any obsessing entity must depart or
be consumed. Get this fact firmly fixed in mind,
that *the desire for drink is not yours*, but that of a
departed drunkard. Also that you have the power
to protect yourself *if you will*."[9]

It is depraved excarnate human beings such as
are described in this chapter and the next who are
the basis of the many descriptions of evil and lying spirits and demons—demons of drink, gluttony,
greed, craft, lust and cruelty—given in the *Bible*
and other scriptures. Some of these creatures are
well represented in the stage version of *Peer Gynt*.
It is also just these influences that are responsible
for the periodic outbreaks of witchcraft, sorcery
and devil worship which sweep whole communities
with cyclones of evil.

It is also largely the influences from this Realm,
together with antagonistic thought-forces from
persons still in the flesh, which constitute the "ma-
licious animal magnetism" which Mrs. Eddy and
the Christian Scientists so greatly fear, because they
do not understand or know how to control.

---

[9] "I think it is a part of my duty to write on behalf of the Christian Mystics,
telling the good I have derived from them, both physically and spiritually.
In plain words I had tried all sources physically for health, and to stop my
vice, drunkenness. And when all others failed me the only place I got relief
was the Christian Mystics, as by following their teachings I have completely
conquered the drink habit." From a pupil in Kingston, Jamaica. The same rules
apply to discarnate narcotic drug addicts. See Appendix.

CHAPTER XI

THE DESIRE REALM

OBSESSING ENTITIES (*Continued*)

"Vice is a monster of so frightful mien,
As to be hated needs but to be seen;
Yet, seen too oft, alas and grown familiar with her face,
We first endure, then pity, then embrace."

An Essay on Man, Pope.

IN this dense region of the Desire Realm there is a third great class of obsessing entities, and also swirling currents of perverted thought and creative forces which sweep over humanity like black thunder storms and hurricanes of evil. Therefore, although this is the most disagreeable phase of the Astral World to discuss, nevertheless because of its everpresent dangers through which the evolving Soul must pass on its journey to the Hall of Wisdom, it is our duty to indicate the character of its denizens and forces and how they may be avoided or overcome.

This third class comprises those who, while on earth, used their human intellects to enhance and gratify their normal and then their perverted animal desires. Hence in this class lust is the ruling passion instead of drink or crime as in the two classes already described, although both of those classes also seek this form of gratification as a secondary object. In this Realm such entities must experience the effects of the causes engendered while on earth, for only thus can they truly learn that "the wages of sin is death."

The occult student, of course, understands that the suffering endured in this Realm is not *eternal* punishment for any individual Soul, as the orthodox believe, for the individual is ultimately purged of his evil and passes on into the higher Realms. "For thou wilt not leave my soul in hell; neither wilt thou suffer thine Holy One to see corruption."[1] The suffering lasts only until the fires of passion and desire have burned themselves out or until the Soul, through sincere repentance, reform, spiritual aspiration and a purification of the mind is able to conquer passion and desire and rise above them. Such conditions of burning and disintegration are eternal in that they will last as long as there is anything false or evil to be consumed.

Believing that life consists of sensation and gratified desire, such entities haunt both dens of vice on earth and also those whose impure thoughts give these entities an opening through which to enter the aura and steal the life-force of their victims, that they may prolong what seems to them the only life and thus escape the approaching disintegration that appears to them to be annihilation. The great

---

[1] *Psalms*, xvi, 10.

danger to the living is that this Realm overlaps and is closest to the physical, hence many persons dwell in it much of the time who do not consider themselves impure and who would be horrified and shocked could they realize into what astral company their impure thoughts and uncontrolled desires led them.

In many cases of melancholia the mind is dwelling in this Realm. For when such thoughts are entertained they open the aura and the consciousness to the influence, suggestions and forces of the entities in this Realm. Yet the purification and control of thought is even more important in the Astral World than in the Physical World, because of the more immediate and powerful results. For when such thoughts are entertained in the Astral World the corresponding forces rush in and make that person almost immediately the astral embodiment of those loathsome evils.

It must be remembered that the spiritual Creative Force is not sex-force, but the Divine life-force which gives sex-force its creative power. That is, it becomes or manifests as sex-force only when a stream or current of it finds expression through the sex centers or is focussed there by thought. If this ever-flowing stream of Creative Force is not utilized in various forms of mental or other creative activity it gradually accumulates, fills the aura and tends to overflow through the sex centers as the points of least resistance. The balance and adjustment of this force should naturally be brought about between man and wife through normal relations in love and purity.

But where this relation cannot be entered into by both in harmony, love and purity of thought also among those who are unmarried—the remedy is neither its expression through the sex centers nor its suppression, *but its diversion into other channels* of creative activity, as fully described in our *Letters from the Teacher*.[2] Where this is not done the aura becomes so overcharged with it that it attracts the class of evil astral entities to which we refer in this lesson. These entities once having gained entrance to the aura, usually over the line of ambition, vanity, sex desire, etc., absorb the life-force and sap the vitality to prolong their lives and carry out their evil designs. Having made the contact with the victim *they constantly stimulate* his sex passions by bringing before his mental vision suggestions, images and thoughts of lust. *Response* to such thoughts and suggestions makes progressive obsession a fairly easy matter, but *resistance* to them, with a sincere desire and determined will to conquer, together with a prayer to The Christ-light within for help, makes such obsession impossible; for prayer or spiritual aspiration invokes forces which dissolve evil thought forms as the sunlight dissipates fog.

Wherever response to their evil suggestions is found, these entities throw a glamor of illusion over the victim, in many cases presenting themselves as

---

[2] Pages 203-5.

high spiritual teachers or as advanced Souls needing merely the victim's magnetism; perhaps as a husband or wife of a former incarnation; as a Soul-mate or under the guise of some living person with whom the victim is in love or who has attracted his or her attention or who has perhaps innocently aroused thoughts of lust. But no matter how high-sounding the excuse or how plausible the sophistry by which they gain the confidence of the victim and entrance to the aura, *the sex idea will ultimately be presented in some form* and that force be drawn upon. Sometimes after this has been accomplished, and nearly always upon challenge, the glamor is dispelled and the true nature of the entity is revealed. This usually brings a revulsion of feeling and a sincere remorse which may protect the victim from temptation for a time, but if the creative forces are not *diverted from* the sex centers and utilized elsewhere, when they again accumulate he is open to a repetition of the same revolting experience, unless in the meantime he has learned to purify and control his thoughts and absolutely close the door of his aura to all such temptations and suggestions.

Especially are the above temptations and suggestions apt to be presented to the student who is seeking to lead the higher life; for he has deliberately turned away from the old thoughts, indulgences and habits of life and set a new and higher standard, especially of purity, and his old thought-forms and temptations strive to drag him down to indulge them

again. Also, having set this higher standard he
thereby invokes the Great Law to prove his
statements; prove whether or not he really means
what he says and has the will and has gained the
power to resist and overcome. This purifying
and testing is well illustrated by the temptations
described by Saint Anthony.

It is well known that light attracts the creatures of the darkness, like moths around a flame,
hence, as the Neophyte's purified aura begins to
shine out it attracts the attention of the evil entities. Furthermore his very spiritual advance has
made him more sensitive to thought influence and
to the Astral World. Therefore, that such temptations should come upon the Neophyte after his
period of exaltation and spiritual realization, is not
a sign that he is falling away from his ideals and
is degenerating, but is an evidence that the growth
he has made is being tested as to just how solid
and enduring it is. No matter how many times he
may be overcome and fail, let him *put his failures
behind him* and determine to *try harder next time*,
remembering the real nature of the entity who
seduced him, and also his own power to gather
out of the burning the force of The Christ with
which to overcome in the future. He should never
mourn or even pray over his failures, for to do so
is to dwell upon them and strengthen them by his
thought-force. Rather let him rouse his slumbering
will to the fighting pitch and determine that next

time he will conquer, then put the matter entirely out of mind and shut the door upon it.

We have used the masculine pronouns in this lesson merely for literary convenience and not because only men are so tempted and obsessed; for we are sorry to say that quite as many, if not more, women are led to indulge their impure thoughts in this way. Hence all we say herein applies equally to women and to men. In fact, being more sensitive to astral influences, women would be more easily seduced by astral entities were it not that their intuition is more developed and is quicker to recognize the nature of the temptations than it is in man. Many, however, who are somewhat psychic plainly see the obsessing entity and call him their "astral lover, spirit-mate or spirit-husband," etc., under the delusion that any truly spiritual being in the higher realms needs either physical magnetism or sex-force. It is just such influences as these that inculcate ideas of so-called "sex freedom" which inevitably result in some form of illicit or "free-love." And it is just such ideas and teachings that the teachings of the Order of Christian Mystics most strenuously oppose, even as a philosophic conception, knowing as it does the utter falsity of such doctrines.[3]

---

[3] See *The Voice of Isis*, Curtiss, Chapters XVI, XVIII, XIX, XXV. *Letters from the Teacher*, Curtiss, Chapter IX. The *Key to the Universe*, Curtiss, pages 345, 282-3, and Appendix.

The compelling influence of this phase of the Desire
Realm is not brought about suddenly, but like that
of the other Realms is of gradual growth. It begins
as a vague desire, then as this desire is yielded to
and the person responds to the suggestions of the
astral influence, his own desires—which normally
he might control—are augmented by the desires
of the astral entities and mere suggestions grow
rapidly into definite and overmastering currents of
thought. As such lustful thoughts are entertained
their power grows stronger until they result in actual
expression and gratification and finally in actual
obsession and bodily control by the astral entity.
These teachings are fully corroborated by Jesus and
St. Paul in the *Bible*, by Paracelsus, Swedenborg,
Jacob Boehme and others among the older writers
and by the venerable spiritualist, Dr. Peebles—than
whom no one is in a better position to know the
reality of the horrors of spirit obsession—and many
others among living authorities. If any are skeptical
as to the reality of these conditions or think we
are merely perpetuating superstition, let them read
Dr. Hartman's *Paracelsus* or Dr. Peebles' *Spirit
Obsessions* in which Dr. Peebles says: "Doubtless
nineteen-twentieths of all intelligent Spiritualists
believe in demoniacal obsessions; that is, *psychic
influences from evil-disposed spirits.* . . . They
also follow and if possible co-mingle their
psychic emanations with certain mortals, and
cling to them as fungus and moss to trees, thus

vampire-like, absorbing their vitality."[4] We are, therefore, neither spreading superstition nor inculcating fear, for we give plain and simple directions how to prevent such influences or obsessions and also how to conquer and drive them away when present.

Our teachings are, therefore, not merely academic and informing, but are vitally *constructive* and *fear eradicating*.

We see that these conditions result from two chief causes, first the suppression or *lack of diversion* of the Creative Force into normal channels *away from* the sex centers, and, second, from *entertaining* and *dwelling upon* impure thoughts and lustful desires. No one in everyday life in the world can entirely prevent such suggestive thoughts from being presented to his consciousness, any more than he can prevent unpleasant sights and inharmonious sounds being presented to his eyes and ears while passing through the streets. The point is—and this is most important to realize clearly—*they need not be entertained* when presented, but can be instantly dismissed. Our glance may present to us the contents of the gutter as we pass, but we do not need to feast our eyes upon it. We can look beyond it and ignore it, or better still, report it and have it removed. We may have to cross the manhole of a sewer, but we do not have to stop and inhale its noxious odors. Our ears may overhear a lewd joke or suggestive

---

[4] *Spirit Obsessions*, 9, iv.

song, but we do not have to remain where such things are going on, or remember or gloat over them. Just so with the evil thoughts and lewd suggestions and lustful desires presented to our consciousness from either the Astral or Physical Worlds. Impress this idea strongly upon your mind. *You do not have to entertain them*, give them lodgment and allow them to grow and develop until they force you to express and gratify them.

Remember that a fundamental law of psychology tells us that "every thought entertained *tends to express itself in terms of action*, unless counteracted by a contrary thought of equal power."

This law applies to all suggestions either from without or within. Those which are entertained tend to result in action. For instance, the carrying of a revolver suggests the right to kill at your discretion, and the temptation to do so is continually present, only waiting the opportunity for expression. We should, therefore, not only resist temptations to respond to suggestions which we do not wish to execute *but should take pains to avoid placing ourselves in positions where such temptations are suggested*. It is difficult for many to resist such temptations because through indulgence in past lives they have been born in this life with weakened wills, lack of self-control and with psychopathic tendencies in general, for the parents with whom they have chosen to incarnate furnished them a body which is either more or less defective or which has an unstable nervous organism. Those who refuse to learn and refuse to exercise self-discipline in this life will lay the foundation for psychopathic and paranoid conditions in a future life. In this respect at least, universal military training—even if not actual service in war—will do much for the regeneration of the Race. For under such training the Soul will be taught the principles of discipline, *i.e.,* obedience, self-sacrifice for an ideal, respect for an authority and proved talent, consideration for others, personal hygienics, etc., all of which will be a tremendous aid to self-discipline after the period of service is over.

The so-called cases of dual and multiple personalities which so greatly puzzle our modern day psychologists, *in most cases* are simply temporary obsessions by various disembodied personalities, although there are certain exceptions too technical to be described here. Rather than admit this simple and almost self-evident fact, recognized throughout the ages, even by Jesus and all the Great Teachers, our modern psychologists—few if any of whom are psychic, have developed any psychic powers or have any *personal knowledge* of psychic experiences, although they still *claim* to be psychologists!— have concocted the most elaborate imaginings as to the splitting up of the one personality into various secondary selves, etc., which require a far greater demand upon our credulity than to admit the simple fact of obsession and control by an astral entity.

As St. John tells us: "We wrestle not against

flesh and blood, but against principalities, against powers, against rulers of the darkness of this world, against spiritual wickedness in high places (Astral World)."[5]

In the Desire Realm all these forces are represented, and are gathered together in what may well be called principalities, with their rulers, satraps and servitors, all prepared to rush forth and fight in every way possible to uphold their rule. And it is these concentrated forces of evil against which we must wrestle day and night. Woe to the poor mortal who opens a door, even a tiny crack, to any of the forces thus enumerated. For instance, consider ambition. There is no more powerful principality than the one ruled by ambition. Often a man or woman is working truly and sincerely and following the Christ in humility, when some well meaning friend suggests to them that they are doing great things which are deserving of recognition by the world, or praises them lavishly for doing their duty. At once the door of ambition is unlatched, and as this door hangs ever loose on its hinges, the recipient of the praise may rather enjoy gazing through its portals. But alas, ere they are aware of their danger, an army from the Principality of Ambition rushes through and captures the citadel of their hearts, and they are carried away captive; so it is with all the other principalities when we open the door through harboring or contemplating their characteristic thoughts.

---

[5] *Ephesians*, vi, 12.

Just as there is beauty, sweetness, fragrance and harmony in nature and the world around us, as well as inharmony, disease and decay, so is there beauty, sweetness, love and purity in the Astral World. And these aspects will be presented to our consciousness instead of the evil if we seek for, demand, affinitize ourselves with and entertain them. If we dislike the odors and conditions found in the slums of a city and desire to enjoy pure air, the trees, flowers and birds, we can enjoy them whenever our *desire for them* is strong enough to cause us to leave the slums and seek the parks, fields or woods. And just as there are obsessing entities who would ruin us to gratify their evil desires, so are there loving friends, spiritual teachers and currents of life-giving spiritual force which will help and uplift us if we correlate with them according to the *independent method* described later.[6] But neither these friends, teachers or forces can reach us while we are surrounded by dark clouds of anger, passion, selfishness or lustful thoughts, nor can they force their way to our side as long as we entertain the crowds of debauched astral entities or perverted teachers which surround us under such conditions. It is for us to choose which class of thoughts and associates we will entertain in the Astral World, just as we choose our associates in the Physical World.

The remedy for overcoming such conditions is the

---

[6] See page 225.

same as for obsession by the two classes mentioned in the former chapter, *i.e.*, the *fearless and positive Challenge* "In the name of The Christ," and the determined invocation of the Divine Fire and Light of The Christ, in the presence of which no thing of darkness or evil can exist. But in addition to the Challenge, in this case you should say to yourself again and again: "I refuse to create! I refuse to create! I refuse to create!" Especially should young persons who are having trouble in controlling their thoughts and desires impress these words upon their subconscious mind just before dropping to sleep; for it is thus possible to train the subconscious mind to wake up and dispel such forces and entities the moment they approach your aura, even while asleep. Also hold the idea of closing a door in your mind and your aura which will shut out all such thoughts and suggestions as soon as they attempt to intrude. For remember, *you do not have to entertain them.*

Another way to protect yourself is to live in such perfect accord with The Christ and dwell so continually in the thoughts of love, purity and un-selfishness, and occupy your mind so fully with earnest thoughts of higher things and with study on these subjects that all obscene thoughts or sugges-tions will be repugnant to you. You will then turn from them as naturally as you would step over a pud-dle of mud in the street. We cannot be absorbed in two things at once, or as Jesus said, we cannot serve two masters, for we will hold to the one and despise the other. Therefore if the general trend of your mind and desire is for higher things do not be distressed if the thing you despised occasionally sweeps over your consciousness, for if you do not serve it, it can never become your master. If Christ is your Master you will so despise the evil that it can and will make little impression upon your mind.

Students who are having special trouble along these lines should immediately put these instructions into practice and if, after a thorough trial, they still have trouble, they may write to the Teacher of the Order of Christian Mystics for more detailed directions. But remember you will never reach a point where vigilance is not necessary. "Guard thou the door of thy heart."

CHAPTER XII

THE EIGHTH SPHERE

"It is better for thee to enter into the Kingdom of God with one eye, than having two eyes to be cast into hell fire: Where their worm dieth not, and the fire is not quenched."

St. Mark, ix, 47-8.

BETWEEN each of the Realms of the Astral World there is an intermediate state which might be compared to an ante-room of the next succeeding Realm. The same thing exists between the Physical World and the Astral World. This overlapping may be compared to the dark shadow of the earth stealing over the sun during an eclipse. Being the lowest of all, the Desire Realm touches the earth at its darkest point, and this overlapping forms an intermediate region (see diagram on page 181) into which the offscourings of both the Physical and Astral Worlds are gathered. This region therefore contains the blackest thought forces and most of the evil entities and conditions created by man which he has been unable to redeem and which therefore must be purified by the fires of disintegration. Here the atmosphere is formed by the foul odors and noxious gases arising from decay and disintegration in both the Physical and Astral Worlds, as well as the effluvia cast off by mankind.

As we have said elsewhere, "This is the outer
darkness into which the unprofitable servant is
cast, which simply means that all the matter which
should be the servant of its Lord (The Christ),
but which fails to respond during one period of
manifestation, must pass through a period of outer
darkness or lie in the grave until the resurrection or
the dawn of the next Manvantara (world period). In
many respects the darkness might be compared to a
compost heap into which all refuse, effete and unus-
able matter is cast, there to ferment in darkness until
the next springtime when it can be spread upon the
earth and its life-force, transmuted by the powers of
the elements, can be utilized to bring forth flowers,
fruits and grains for the service and sustenance of
man. This accumulated mass is darkness because it
is composed of dead matter, incapable of reflecting
light. . . . Like the darkness of Chaos, it is preg-
nant with the germs of that which must ultimately
come into the light and be redeemed by its creator."[1]

In the Desire Realm a dim and brooding twilight
forms its daylight, and oppressive darkness its night.
But in this overlapping ante-chamber its brightest
day is a murky and clammy darkness, while its night
is a period of dense, impenetrable blackness which
is beyond the power of mortals to describe. It is a
night beyond earthly conception; indeed, it is well

---

[1] *The Voice of Isis*, Curtiss, page 323.

described as "the outer darkness." The blackness
is so dense and heavy that it surrounds those
unfortunate enough to enter it and oppresses them
as with the weight of centuries. They feel as though
wedged in between mountains, yet all the time there
is a sense of being alive and surrounded with horror
unspeakable.

This answers the question so frequently asked as
to why man, although created a pure and perfect being made in the image of God, should be subjected
almost from the beginning to the temptation of dis-
obedience and evil. He has to take up and redeem
all his creations that have been left over from past
world periods. It is the influence of these old creations of his that tempts him to continue their life
by repeating the same old mistakes. This temptation
in the *Bible* allegory is called the serpent which
was already in the Garden before man appeared,
i.e., matter impregnated with his old creations and
mistakes awaiting his coming for their redemption.

This intervening region is called the Eighth
Sphere, both because it is an addition to the seven-
fold chain of globes constituting the Earth Chain,
and because it is a double four or the point where the
foundation of one sphere (earth) is merging into the
foundation on which a better and higher planet will
be built. For just as the effluvia of decay is transmitted into gas and then into new and useful products, so
the deep repentance and realization of mistakes and
crimes committed on earth are here made the foun-

dation on which a new humanity can be brought forth.

In this sphere are found those soulless mortals whose persistent refusal to respond to the guidance of the Higher Self through many lives or to listen to the voice of conscience, have thereby atrophied the centers and avenues through and over which that guidance reaches the body and impinges upon the consciousness. When the atrophy of these channels of communication is complete the human personality breaks away from the overshadowing Soul or Higher Self and becomes but a soulless, hence conscienceless human animal. Such persons are not "lost souls," for the Soul is immortal and cannot be "lost," but they are lost human animals, for it is the personality only that is lost, not the Soul. These soulless beings are the "Jack the Rippers"—beings without a single redeeming trait—who commit the most atrocious and revolting crimes without a pang of conscience or remorse. They cannot feel remorse for the Soul whose chiding causes the remorse has abandoned them. At death such persons pass into the blackness of this Eighth Sphere where they dwell continually surrounded by their crimes and often continually fleeing defiantly but hopelessly from the retribution they fear, and which they imagine is pursuing them, as in the case of a man with a rope around his neck described in a remarkable communication from the Astral World in 1851.[2]

[2] *Letters from Hell*, pages 13-14.

A creature is described who "had a rope around its neck, the hands being constantly trying to secure the ends." He is made to say "I am for ever trying to escape; there is not a creature but wants to hang me. . . . It is my one aim to prevent people getting hold of them. . . . whenever this foolish fear possesses me afresh, I must run, run as though I had a thousand lives to lose."

Other dwellers in this region may remain chained in consciousness to their victims. In many cases their crime was the result of obsession, and now that they are freed from that obsession they are brought face to face with the crimes and must realize their responsibility.

Here also dwell the soulless monsters of lust who while on earth have persistently and knowingly perverted the currents of Creative Force as it manifests through the sex centers. To correctly understand the condition in which the denizens of this region dwell we must remember that the sex-force is *but one manifestation* of the Divine Life-essence or the Great Creative Force which is eternally bringing all manifested things into existence and whose unceasing onward and upward urge is the force back of all evolution, forever transmuting matter into Spirit and ever seeking higher forms of expression. This Force is a living unquenchable Divine Fire which should integrate, build up and perfect, but which just as truly consumes the false and impure, that the Life-essence which has been perverted may be released and used for man's ultimate redemption.

It is this Divine Fire of The Christ-force that is referred to so frequently in the New Testament. "He shall baptize you with the Holy Ghost and with fire. . . . And he will thoroughly purge his floor, and gather his wheat into the garner; but he will burn up the chaff with unquenchable fire." In another place we are told that "The Lord thy God is a consuming fire," etc. This Realm, therefore, bears a close resemblance to the orthodox conceptions of hell so graphically described in Dante's *Inferno*, "Where the worm dieth not, and the fire is not quenched." The "worm" is the continued gnawing of evil desires which in this region have no means of gratification, not even through obsessing sensitive mortals still living in the flesh as do those in the Desire Realm. The "worm" therefore is the continual disappointment, anger and suffering arising from pursuing the tantalus of expectations and fierce desires forever unfulfilled. The unquenchable fire is the Divine Fire of The Christ-force which slowly burns out the dross of impurity and ultimately disintegrates and consumes everything that prevents its manifestation in purity and truth, that the life currents may flow along normal and constructive lines.

The entities of this region therefore suffer both because they cannot gratify their fierce desires and also because they realize, even if vaguely, that their astral bodies are being slowly consumed. They still have sufficient intelligence to realize something of the horror of their condition and the dread of the ultimate destiny which they more or less vaguely sense. Such a state of consciousness is truly all that has been pictured by the orthodox conceptions of hell.

It is into this region that suicides precipitate themselves when they refuse to live out their appointed time on earth. "When, through vice, fearful crimes and animal passions, a disembodied spirit has fallen to the Eighth Sphere—the allegorical Hades, and the gehenna of the *Bible*—the nearest to our earth—he can with the help of that glimpse of reason and consciousness left to him, repent; that is to say, he can, by exercising the remnants of his will-power, strive upward, and like a drowning man, struggle once more to the surface. . . . A strong aspiration to retrieve his calamities, a pronounced desire, will draw him once more into the earth's atmosphere. Here he will wander and suffer more or less in dreary solitude. His instincts will make him seek with avidity contact with living persons. These spirits are the invisible but too tangible magnetic vampires; the *subjective* demons so well known to medieval ecstatics, nuns, and monks, to the 'witches' made so famous in the *Witch-Hammer*; and to certain sensitive clairvoyants, according to their own confessions. . . . It is because Moses knew so well what they were, and how terrible were the consequences to weak persons who yielded to their influence, that he

enacted the cruel, murderous law against such
would-be 'witches;' but Jesus, full of justice and
divine love to humanity, healed instead of killing
them. Subsequently our clergy, the pretended
exemplars of Christian principles, followed the
law of Moses, and quietly ignored the law of Him
whom they call their 'one living God,' by burning
dozens of thousands of such pretended 'witches,'[3]
i.e., obsessed mortals.

Although they find themselves in this region of
the soulless the case of suicides is quite different
from that of the entities described above, although
they are in a most pitiable condition and suffer
most terribly. They pass out in such a depressed,
despondent or insane state of mind that the terrible thoughts, gnawing sorrow and despair which
caused the deed surround them like a shell or pall
of black horror. This envelopes them so completely
and is so dense that neither their spirit friends nor
the spiritual helpers can reach them with their help
until they make an opening in this black aura, either
by sincere repentance or a definite aspiration for the
Christ-light. Had they resisted the impulse to suicide
and remained in the body the black mood and darkest despair would have passed away in a few hours
or at least in a few days and been outlived and new
conditions would have presented themselves, but
now since they are continually surrounded by the

---

[3] *Isis Unveiled*, Blavatsky, ii, 352-3.

same black thoughts which prompted the deed, they are impelled to reenact the scene over and over again, for they continue to live in the moment at which the deed was done. Since there is no division of time in this region, as we have it on earth, the duration of time is marked only by sensation and so long as these sensations endure time stands still and their despair seems endless, for no other moment can be experienced until the old sensations are worked out and exhausted and new sensations can be experienced.

Since they have refused to be comforted by time's healing hand, and as the allotted amount of life-force they were originally able to bring with them into incarnation has not been exhausted either by living or used up by sickness, they are not ready to enter the normal astral life. And since they have refused to go on with the Physical World they find the door is shut in both directions. And like a child who has run away from its tasks and shut itself in a dark closet, they realize that they are absolutely and terribly alone; that they are not in the Realms with their departed friends, neither can they return to earth, but are shut in with only the memory of their despair and the dreadful deed they have committed. This, however, is not a cruel punishment, for only as they realize to its bitterest extreme what it means to take their own lives, can it be so deeply imprinted on their consciousness that in no future life will they repeat the deed, for when the similar

impulse comes at a corresponding period in the next
life—for come it must since the experiences leading
up to the deed must be met again and again until
conquered—there will be such an inward horror
that they will have gained (except in extreme cases)
the strength of character to face conditions, resist
the impulse and conquer it. But, unlike the case of
soulless entities, there is hope; for as soon as the
Soul really repents, which is quite different from
merely being sorry, a ray of Light will be shown
him, and if he follows this it will lead him out of
this "outer darkness" into the region of the Astral
World to which he is otherwise affinitized. There
are organized bands of nurses in the lower Realms
who are especially trained to help such cases, for
they are too dangerous for the ordinary dweller in
the astral to have anything to do with, even if such
should penetrate into this outer darkness.

Suicides realize that they are absolutely and
terribly alone and so seek the companionship of
those left behind and naturally throw over them
the same pall of depression which overwhelmed
them, so that the one whom they approach feels
impelled to commit suicide in the same way, although the mere approach of the suicide to his
friends tends to throw his condition over them
quite unconsciously to himself. We have had
several students corroborate this teaching from
their own experience. In some cases the loneliness and remorse of the suicide is so terrible that
he deliberately obsesses some mortal and tries to

get him to commit suicide, usually in the same manner, hoping thereby to gain his companionship. But even if such an obsession is successful, as it frequently is, the suicide is still disappointed and alone, for he is shut away from his victim more than before. The main thing to be remembered about suicide is that *it never relieves the victim* from the mental depression and suffering which he seeks to escape, but prolongs and *increases it a thousandfold.*

CHAPTER XIII.

THE ELEMENTALS

"Substantial but (for us) invisible beings of an ethereal nature, living in the elements of air, water, earth, or fire. They have no immortal spirits, but. . . . are of various grades of intelligence."

Paracelsus, Hartman, 44.

"Whether the results produced are styled miraculous or not, depends on our knowledge — our knowledge of all the powers latent in nature, and a knowledge of all the intelligences which exist."

Raymond, Lodge, 318.

IT is the intermediate states previously referred to as existing between the various Realms that are the abiding place of most of the kingdoms, races and tribes of tiny beings called Elementals.

Matter, force and consciousness is a trinity that is found everywhere in nature inseparably blended. Therefore, not only does every form of matter have a consciousness of its own, but also every force in nature has a form of consciousness in its own Realm. These forces are entitized in various forms of life called by the general term of Elementals. And as few people, even among occult students have a clear idea of what is meant by the term, we will endeavour to make the subject somewhat clearer in these pages.

The Elementals are the various orders of entitized nature forces which, obeying the will of the creative Hierarchies, bring into material manifestation the details of the Grand Plan of the Universe. In other words they are the means by which the Divine Life-essence expresses the ideals in the Divine Mind through form, hence they are the intelligences whose manifestation bring about the normal flow of the earth currents and the activities of nature.

There is a wide range between the various manifestations of these forces, but in general they are divided into four great kingdoms, each under the direction of a great Master belonging to one of the creative Hierarchies. These four kingdoms are the Earth, whose elementals are called Gnomes; Water, whose elementals are the Undines; Air, whose elementals are the Sylphs, and the Fire, whose elementals are the Salamanders. Each of these four divisions are broken up into many tribes and races, each with its own characteristics. We find them referred to everywhere in literature under various names; in fact, almost every country and every language has its folk-lore in which these elementals figure under various terms, yet all can be classified under these four main divisions. In each of the four kingdoms there are elementals of varying degrees of consciousness and intelligence, varying from the true Nature Sprites or rulers of their kingdoms, down to the rudimentary lives over which they rule.

These rudimentary elemental lives are the very essence of the physical substances themselves and their life manifestations give to the various forms of matter their chemical properties. There is almost as great a difference in form and consciousness between the Nature Sprites and the rudimentary elemental lives as there is between man and the insects. While man, being the Lord of Creation, lives in all of the four elements—earth, air, water and solar fire or heat—the elementals live exclusively in one element. The conditions of each element are as normal to its inhabitants as physical conditions are to man. For instance, to the Gnomes the earth is transparent and offers no bar to their progress or activities, while the Salamanders live as naturally in fire as man does in air.

Beside the four great classes of elementals, there is a class which although elemental differs widely from those already described. As we have stated in a previous Chapter, there are soulless beings who have broken away from the informing Ego. These beings after a few incarnations on earth,[1] exhaust every remnant of the informing Soul's life-force and reach a point where the atoms composing their astral bodies are disintegrated in the Eighth Sphere. After such disintegration, since in the great economy of nature nothing is lost, the elements composing those bodies must again start on the long "cycle of necessity" and pass through all the stages of experience

[1] *The Voice of Isis*, Curtiss, page 99.

as elemental forces in nature, passing through the mineral, vegetable, etc. Hence in this region of the elementals, the forces once composing those bodies have reached a state where they have become elementals, but they differ from Nature Sprites in that the substance of their forms has once existed in human bodies, while the Nature Sprites animate only the elements. This class of elementals are the rudimentary and lowest astral forms of future man. Here in this Realm the monad must evolve through the nature states until taken up and built into the human kingdom as molecules in the lowest form of physical man. The Soul which once broke away from the body must again gather these forces and atoms together and build new bodies which it can inform.

All four classes of Nature Sprites are made in the miniature image of man. Some, such as the Gnomes, are often distorted and grotesque, but the Sprites of the other kingdoms are more beautiful, dainty and fairy-like. Indeed they are the fairies themselves. In many cases it is such elementals and mischievous Nature Sprites, especially the Gnomes, who impersonate the departed at a séance, for they delight in their power to deceive and play all kinds of pranks on both the medium and the sitter. The Nature Sprites belong to the highest races of each great kingdom, but the subject is so vast that in this work we must confine our few subsequent remarks to the four classes of Nature Sprites only.

Among them we find a vast number of races and tribes varying as widely as do the several races and tribes of mankind. And just as with man, each tribe has its home in a certain locality on earth and is largely confined to that region. For instance, every region of earth, such as mountain, valley, or plain has its own particular tribes of Gnomes which are not found in any other part of the globe. In the same way every form of water, babbling brook, meadow stream, broad river, lake, sea or ocean has its particular tribe of Undines. The air also has its many races of Sylphs. Every type of wind, from the gentle zephyrs of summer and the steady trade winds, the winds of land and sea, to the storm winds and tornados, have their own characteristic tribes.

For instance, among the Gnomes there is a race of gold elementals to which belong all the tribes connected with the various deposits of gold in different parts of the world. Another race is composed of all the tribes connected with copper, and so on for each metal, rock and earth. Gold being the highest metal, the tribes of all other metals are subservient to its rulers, the gold Gnomes. There are other tribes belonging to the vegetable kingdoms which guide the elemental lives in building up the grass, the trees, the flowers, etc. It is because the people who live for a long time in one locality imbibe and have built into their bodies, through the food they eat, the water they drink and the air they breathe, etc., the elemental forces of that locality, that they

take on the peculiarities of that region and feel at
home there. Persons who do not live in one place
long have their elemental forces so mixed that they
feel no especial attraction for any one locality.

While the elemental forces of all four kingdoms
are more or less responsive to man's thoughts and
desire forces, only the more advanced, such as the
Nature Sprites, are sufficiently individualized to
communicate with man under certain conditions,
as we find witnessed to in the literature, philosophy
and religion of all ages and among all peoples. It
is not that these Sprites speak to man in English,
French, German, Japanese, etc., but rather that
certain sensitive mortals are able to attune their
consciousness to that of the Sprites and then express
that consciousness in the best words their mentality
is able to use. It is easiest for man thus to communicate with the Gnomes, as they are closest to man
and most easily made friends with, while communion with the Undines and Sylphs is more difficult.
It is the most difficult of all for man to communicate
with the Salamanders, for with few exceptions they
are antagonistic to man unless he has in a measure
been able to enter consciously into their kingdom,
in which case they will be his obedient servants. In
fact, all the elementals obey man when he can prove
to them his superiority. But since they obey and
recognize forces rather than the mere form of man,
the man who would dominate the elementals, either
for good or evil must be forceful; must prove his

ability to rule. This is more effectively done, however, through real love and understanding of their true nature than through mere will power.

American Indians in the Astral World, being earth children and living so close to nature, are in very close touch with the Gnomes and earth elementals. In fact, those of them who earnestly desire to help in the great work of evolution, and there are many such, use their human intelligence to tutor the rulers of the earth elementals, even lending to them the power of speech so that such rulers may come into contact with those upon the earth plane who could aid them by bringing them in contact with and implanting in them love and brotherhood from the human kingdoms. For the elementals obey man's thought, and work it out in their own kingdom. Evil elementals are but elementals instinctively working out man's evil thoughts, either in a vague way, bringing pestilence and disaster, or in a more definite way if the evil is given forth by a strong mentality, one who attracts these forces strongly and commands them to work out definite evil ends.

CHAPTER XIV

THE FAIRIES

"And hark, the many-voiced earth,
The chanting of the old religious trees,
Rustle of far off waters, woven sounds
Of small and multitudinous lives awake,
Peopling the grasses and the pools with joy,
Uttering their meaning to the mystic night."
                    Pyrrha in Moody's *Fire Binger.*

IN describing certain regions and Realms of
the Astral World we have been obliged to refer to
many very disagreeable subjects and conditions,
but it should be remembered that such regions and
conditions form but a limited portion of that World.
That the student may have some realization of the
beauties of other regions, and also to show what
inspiring ideas may be gained by correlating our
human consciousness with the consciousness of the
elementals of the higher orders, we give herewith
some characteristic communications from them. It
is understood, of course, that the Sprites indicated
did not say the exact words given. The words are
simply the best words the mentality of the authors
could find to express both the rhythm and the ideas to
which their consciousness responded as they corre-

lated with those intelligences. Such communications always have their characteristic weird yet musical rhythm, but no attempt has been made to give them polished literary form.

From our investigations and experience we are convinced that in many cases the descriptions given of the fairies by poets—as for instance those given by Shakespeare in *Midsummer Night's Dream, The Tempest*, etc.—are simply a reproduction of the consciousness of the various Nature Sprites to which the authors responded, either unconsciously or in many cases consciously.

THE FAIRIES' KISS

(To each of three persons present at the time)

From A Nymph

A kiss upon your lips dear Brother that shall make you speak kind words.

A kiss on the lips for you dear Sister that shall make you speak pure and beautiful words.

A kiss upon the lips of you dear Priestess that shall make you speak for us. For all the Little People shall show to mortals how we are made up; made out of light, sunshine and joy and happiness. When mortals let in our forces then we draw close. And the more light, joy and sunshine and happiness they let in, the more we come and dance in their hearts and shine from out their eyes, till mortals see us dancing in the light, just as you see motes dancing in a sunbeam.

Come thou and dance with us.
Oh, let us happy be!
Mortals with joy be free!
Let us now happy be.
Come, come with me!

From A Salamander

A kiss upon the lips for thee, Brother, that thou
shall speak fiery words of strength and power.

A kiss upon the lips for thee, Sister, that the
strength of Love shall fill thee; that thy lips shall
smile always.

A kiss on the lips for thee, dear Priestess that
the Flame shall manifest in thy heart and life, consuming all the dross and purifying the love that
humanity lays at thy feet.

We have come again
Light of the Flame.
Joy we bring to thee
Out of the Flame.

From A Sylph

A kiss on the lips for you dear Brother, soft as
a zephyr's touch, filling thy heart with tenderness,
filling thy life with joy.

What a kiss on thy lips dear Sister!
Like the wind from Fairyland,
Blowing away all doubts and fears.
    All loneliness throughout the years;
Filling thy life with tenderness,
Wiping away all tears;
        Watching near thee ever, ever,
        Throughout the long, long years.

A kiss on thy lips, dear Priestess. A kiss that
takes not gives. A kiss that is filled with sweetness,
a kiss on which we live. Oh, breathe out thy Spirit
in loving. Oh bind up thy heart in joy. Think only
of the joys of giving; thy years full of love employ.

Life is full of loving
Life is full of joy
Whispers the breeze of loving
Whispering to girl and boy.
Sweet little nestlings are waiting.
The springtime draweth near.
Open thy heart with loving
For the joy of the springtime is here,
For the joy of the springtime is here.

FROM A GNOME

A kiss of Earth to dear Master
    I bring you my wealth and my store.
I have but a pick o'er my shoulder
    But I lay all its gifts at thy door.
A kiss on thy lips dear Sister
    And out of the earth comes cheer,
Plenty and life-giving forces
    To save you from sorrow and fear.
Out of the darkness of winter,
    When the snow and the ice are gone,
The storehouse of Nature shall fill you.
    You shall gather her wealth in your barn.
A kiss on your lips dear Priestess
    Earth's angels are whispering now.
Out of its bosom comes healing,
    Out of its breath comes balm.
Balm for a spirit distracted,
    Life for the flesh ill at ease,
Priestess of mercy and goodness
    The earth brings a blessing to seize.

A GNOME EXPLAINS AN ERUPTION

Down in the ground where the little fairies are,
the Salamanders are lighting the fires, and we fairies see what it all means. There are things in the
earth that burn and burn and burn, and there are
things that move and move and move. And some
day the water drips and drips and drips down into
the fiery depths of the earth where the fire burns
till it is all white hot, with curling, glowing flames
of rosy hue. And there in the depths of this fiery
heart the Fire Elementals live. They mysteriously
move in the depths of the earth. And all the time
they grow and grow and grow, and that which was
once a fairy dell where the innocent little wood
nymphs play now is in the fiery heart. Some day
while the waters drip, a little elemental of water,
full of interest and curiosity, peeks down into this
chamber to see what is going on. Then her sisters
hear her scream and she is swallowed up. Then they
all rush in to save her life. The Fire Elementals clap
their hands and lo the whole hill explodes. And the
trees and grass and insects and birds all go down
into the fiery depths of earth.

A WIND SPRITE SPEAKS

I know the Masters of the World. I helped them
build their great and beautiful Temple thousands and
millions of years ago. I carried on my magic wings
the great stones. I worked by the power that comes

from the eyes of the great Masters of Wisdom. I can lead you, when They give me their permission to do so, into the secret crypts of the Temple. I have watched and waited and obeyed and known what was intended, because I am part of the elemental power that is used and manipulated to bring about the great changes that the Master in his great wisdom and mighty will desires. I can ride upon the whirlwind. I can fulfill the decrees of the great North-wind. When it sweeps across the prairies, when it shakes the windows of your home, it is I who seek admission. . . . I can make myself at home in the soft murmurs of your dreams. I can whisper of love and of beauty and of peace. When the Master wants his servants to understand, He sends me forth and I embody His thought and am propelled by His will. And so I come to you direct from the eyes of the Master.

CONSECRATION OF THE GOLD

By A Gnome

You want to know the meaning of my domain? How can I tell to mortals or express in mortal language what is not mortal? How can I make them understand? How can I tell them of Sylphs, Undines, Salamanders and Gnomes? . . . How did it happen? Why Great Thor threw into the middle of an immense sea a monstrous mountain. This mountain he shot out with his right hand. When it fell into the waters the Undines were imprisoned. And when they found their domain thus invaded they were in despair. Then the Sylphs of the air rushed in with a mighty voice through passages which the Gnomes had carefully carved to the relief of the imprisoned Undines. With a mighty voice and song of triumph they rushed through the passages so the imprisoned Spirits in the water could breathe as the air rushed hither and thither. Then the Gnomes, good servants as they are to the Sylphs, followed with their picks and shut and plastered up passages and made other passages here and there. None of them knew what they were creating, they only followed their leaders, and they only knew that the Great God had told them to build and plaster up the passages. Then came the grand army of the Salamanders and gathered together all the chips from our work and pressed them to their fiery hearts and evolved a yellow substance, the soul of the earth, a beautiful yellow substance. It was pure and better in this great mountain than in any other place, because it was created through sacrifice in effort to relieve the imprisoned Undines. And when all the Sylphs, Undines, Gnomes and Salamanders had blended their life forces into one, lo! we had a great mountain piled up with gold. And the seed of it grew and grew.

And the great gods came down and looked at our work and pronounced it good, and spake these words, and we engraved them in the heart of the mountain in all its windings and its passages. Again and again we repeated it. "This gold is not to be desecrated or used for the debasement of mankind. It is dedicated to my holy temple." Some day a grand structure will be erected by another order of beings neither Sylph, Undines, Gnomes or Salamanders, but something that contains them all. And these beings (men) shall be the Lords of Creation and all we "little people" shall obey them when they come with a sacred scroll inscribed with the same sacred characters that we have carved in the passages. When they bring us this scroll—it is not a mountain like ours but just a little piece of parchment, yet these beings have traced figures on it, the exact figures we have been all these ages learning and carving within the mountain—when we recognize these figures we will know our masters have come and we will obey them. This gold would be a curse to anyone who should use it for any purpose save that for which it was created. It was created to beautify the Temple of the Sun. This Temple shall be covered over with pure gold. Even now in the regions where we work we can lead you to a passage which shall descend by steps carved out of solid gold. This is the only metal fit to be used in certain parts of the great Temple. That is what gold is created for, to impart its magnetic aura to man and focus the sun-force for the worship of the gods. When it is degraded for barter all the powers of the gods who have been thus insulted let it become a curse to all who touch it. Mankind will learn this lesson only after many ages; after he has suffered from the gold fever. Then he will not abuse gold by using it for such degrading purposes.

TINKLE BUBBLE

A MOUNTAIN WATER SPRITE

Take a book and sit by the brook
And read of the fairies and sylphs
Read of all the beauties you'll find
In my murmuring mountain brook.
This is the home of Tinkle Bubble
Here you will find no trouble
Only joy, only joy, joy, joy.
O, here you'll find no trouble
In the home of Tinkle Bubble.
O little Brother meet me on the shore,
Singing, singing to my home of joy,
Come with me little Brother, little Sister
Come with Tinkle Bubble and forget your earthly trouble
For its joy, joy, joy at the home of Tinkle Bubble,
I will meet you on the shore in the twinkling of an eye.

THE SPIRIT OF THE STORM WIND

I am the Spirit of the Storm Wind that blows the waves; that changes the day to night; that saddens the world and lets the rain from the mighty deep pour over the darkened earth until it is engulfed. Blow, blow, blow ye winds. Blow from the West, blow from the North. Let the ocean find itself a new bed, a new bed. What is so beautiful as the breakers on the shore!

AN UNDINE'S PROPHECY

(Given in June, 1914)

The waters shall cleanse the earth! The dead and dying both alike are carried by the beautiful clear waters of the ocean. The implements of death, misery and suffering are all washed away and the beautiful waters of the ocean with the sunlight on them are moving, moving, so calm and sweet and clean. Breathe in the air, the salt, salt air of the ocean.

What is this putrid smell of unburied thousands? Of earth saturated with blood? What is this death that man has made? It is hideous. It smells aloud to heaven. How horrible! Then the beautiful clear waters come with their sweet breath of purity and life, the salt of purity and sweetness. Smell the air! How sweet it is. This is not death, for there is no death, it is only the Divine Law which goes forth and says: "Go back and be washed by the ocean, be covered up; when purified let the dry land appear." All this land will be filled with forces, little seeds of love and life that have been purified by the waters. And they draw to themselves other forces and out of these little flames of life try to embody themselves in trees and grass and flowers. Then they grow stronger and embody themselves into something else. And after a long, long time God says to man: "Go and dwell on the new land I have made for you.

Then man comes and finds all things growing. Then God says: "These are the things you have made. I have sent my ocean to wash away the wickedness you created by your thoughts. But in your spirit the Divine Life centered and has brought forth."

THE OCEAN IS KING

Onward, onward we go. The ocean is king! The ocean is king! Down, down, down, O, land, underneath the waves. A new day, a new place to play, ye nymphs of the caves! Man, puny creature is gone, and the land where he dwelt and made his proud boast, where is it now? Under the waves! And over it the dolphins dance and play all day. O puny man, where is your kingdom? Would you keep back the great deep? Ha! ha! Onward, onward, over the land. Now it is gone. It is gone. The spray dashes high and the beautiful sun shines through its depths and makes myriads of diamonds and pearls. They are not tears, but pearls of joy, joy, joy, while the dolphins dance and play. For the land is gone, is gone, is gone.

A ROGUISH ELF

Among all the embodied nature forces there is one who reigns supreme; his name is Love. Oh, he is such a roguish elf! He steals into men's hearts and pours out such sweet balm. He seldom talks but just expresses himself in a mystic language known alone to the heart. Have you met him child of earth? Or have you merely met his foster brother who talks and talks until you are weary of his chatter? Yes, and betimes he grows so eloquent with his own glowing word pictures that he forgets others and remembers only himself. Poor thing! Then he suffers and cries out at the gross blindness and inhumanity of the children of men. Have you met him? You may find him easily, but you will know him from his brother, because his brother, Love, seldom speaks when you meet him. He gazes in your face with starry misty eyes and smiles, yet the smile and the look shines in your heart all the day through.

THE FAIRY'S ENCOURAGEMENT

Beloved of Christ keep your Star shining bright
Out through the darkness of earth's dreary night.
Mid toil and confusion of battle and strife,
Send out your message of Love. It is life.

O souls who are patiently waiting for day,
Be not discouraged; turn not away;
For the day that is dawning is gloriously bright;
The dreams so appalling will flee with the night.

Press on, my warriors, fear not the fray.
We are the Conquerors; our Voice obey.
Sound loud the trumpet blast, happy and free,
To tell of the Day Star that is destined to be.

Oh! earth that is sobbing, like a child in its sleep.
Oh! Brothers who suffer with pain fierce and deep.
Stand still in the ruin your passions have wrought
Take count of the guerdon greed and sorrow have
  brought.
If your heart sinks despairing in the mystical calm,
List to God's choir; its echoes bring balm.
The fire but purifies; strife ends in peace.
Hosanna! Hosanna! the carnage must cease.
Lift up your voices, the day is at hand.
No more of sorrow to this happy land.

CHAPTER XV

THE PSYCHIC REALMS

The Mental Realm

"Thou shalt not let thy senses make a playground of thy mind."

The Voice of Silence, Blavatsky.

"It is reasonable to suppose that the mind can be more at home, and more directly and more exuberantly active, when the need for such interaction between psychical and physical no longer exists, when the restraining influence of brain and nerve mechanism is removed."

Raymond, Lodge, 313.

AFTER passing through the experiences and learning the lessons of the four lower Realms, and having purified the body from the denser earth attractions, the Soul dies to the lower Realms, slips off the dense astral body and leaves it behind to disintegrate in the astral graveyards, just as it left the physical body to disintegrate in the tomb.

The four lower Realms of dense astral matter which the Soul now leaves are usually what is referred to when the term Astral World is used, for the reason that it is from these Realms that the forces and phenomena commonly called astral usually come. But there is almost as great a difference between the four lower Realms and the three higher, into which the Soul now enters, as there is between the states of matter constituting the Physical World and the finer states composing the lower astral. Both the latter are states of matter, but of far different rates of vibration. Just so the three higher Realms are composed of astral substance—as distinguished from the *matter* of the lower Realms—but of a far higher rate of vibration and finer condition.

To make this great difference more clearly realized we shall refer to these three higher Realms as the *Psychic Realms*, leaving the term astral to apply to the four lower. We use the specific term *psychic* here because the word itself means Soul and these are truly the Soul Realms, for it is in these Realms that the Soul, freed from the hampering garments of the physical and astral bodies and purified from its lower desires, finds the greatest scope for its most perfect expression in this World. This division may be roughly indicated by the following diagram.

Psychic Realms {
Ecstatic
Inspiration
Mental
}

Astral Realms {
Desire
Vital
Ethereal
Reflection
}

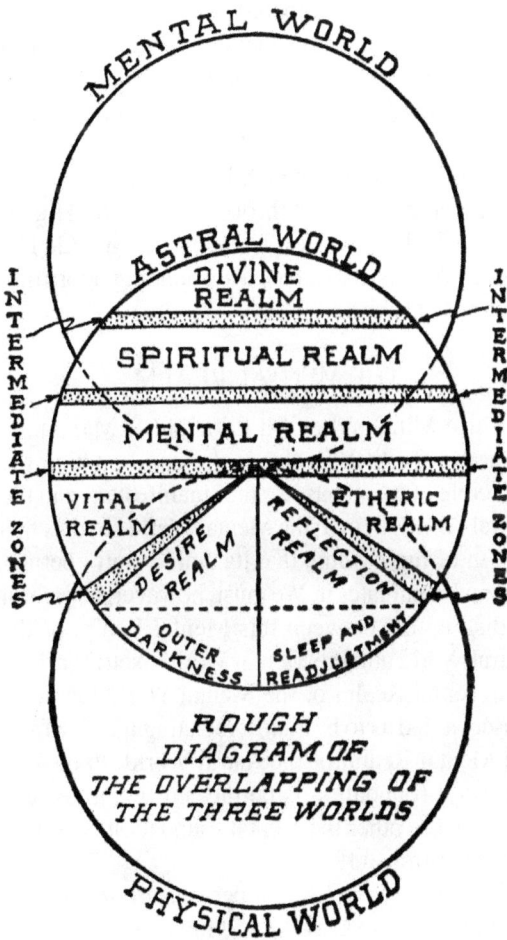

FIGURE 1

Diagram illustrating the overlapping and interpenetration
of the realms of the Astral World and the Physical and
Mental Worlds

It must be remembered, however, that these Realms are all a part of the Astral World and must not be confused with the Higher Worlds beyond, each of which has its seven Realms. Each Astral Realm is astral, yet partakes of the substance of the Higher World to which it is affinitized, hence is the vehicle or door through which the Higher Worlds find expression in the Astral World. The Higher Worlds also have corresponding doors into the Physical World.

THE MENTAL REALM

Since Mind is the fifth Principle of Man, quite naturally the fifth Realm is the one in which the Principle of Mind has its chief manifestation in the Astral World. In fact, the Mental World so rules this Realm of the Psychic that its "mind stuff" permeates and dominates it. We must, however, be careful to distinguish between this Mental Realm of the Astral World and the Mental World itself; for there is an Astral Realm of the Mental World that is so closely allied as to be almost indistinguishable from the Mental Realm of the Astral World. In the one the astral foundation is permeated by mind stuff, while in the other the mental foundation is permeated by astral stuff.

Just as very intellectual persons are said to live in the Mental World while still in the physical body, so after leaving the physical body, having very little interest in the phenomena and life of the lower Realms, they quickly gravitate to the Mental Realm of the astral without spending much time or having much experience in the lower Realms. When this occurs the one thus finding himself surrounded by and breathing and living in mind stuff, is apt to be so well pleased, finding his own mentality so greatly stimulated, that for a long period he revels in his mentality, going over and over his pet hobbies of earth and seeing in them deeper and deeper possibilities. But after a time, according to his Soul development, he finds that he is not gaining *new* truths or unfolding *new* avenues of thought, but that only the seed thoughts already sown are sprouting; the avenues already developed are growing deeper and the intellectual acumen pertaining to problems already in his mind is quickening. Here we might say he wears out his old mental experiences and begins to look around him and respond to new ideas, or perhaps enters one of the great schools.

But the average person who is not especially intellectual also reaches and functions in this Realm in the course of his astral evolution. First the earth desires, which hold him to the lower and more material Realms already described, must be worked out in those lower Realms and their earth attraction exhausted. As they are worked out and the denser particles of the astral body are excreted or washed out and left behind, the Soul is ultimately clothed in a purified, etherealized and mentalized astral body of a much finer texture than that used while dwelling in the lower Realms. This we now term the psychic body. This psychic body has been so purified of its earthly elements that it can no longer appear objectively in earth conditions; cannot obsess or become the "control" of a subjective medium or appear in a materializing séance for example, yet it is capable of affecting physical conditions through the power of thought far more powerfully than can those who appear objectively in the lower Realms. It is in a psychic body, therefore, that the Soul dwells in the Psychic Realms of the Astral World.

Sitters in spiritualistic séances are frequently told that their friends have descended to them from higher spheres or, on the other hand, that they were about to pass on into a higher state. In many cases, although not all, this simply means that they have risen from the lower Realms into the more rarefied Psychic Realms. In those cases in which they say they are going on into a Realm from which they cannot return to contact or control the medium, it usually means that they are about to die to the astral body and ascend into the Psychic Realms. The Ethereal Realm is usually the highest Realm reached by the average subjective medium, for by the abnormal subjective method they are unable to reach those who have died to the lower Realms and who hence have no dense astral body with which to descend into the lower Realms and make a physical contact with the medium.

As we have already said elsewhere, when this Mental Realm is entered the attractions of either the lower Realms or of the earth no longer hold the Soul, for in consciousness it is dwelling largely in the Mental World. This condition is so much higher than that of the lower Realms that although *for a time* the Soul can descend into the lower Realms and pass freely back and forth if it so desires, ultimately it may be said to die to the lower astral, after which it cannot return to earth conditions except mentally. When this change takes place the Soul "has passed on into a higher sphere" as the spiritualists express it, in which state it is beyond the reach of the ordinary medium.

While the Mental is a higher Realm, yet it too has its dangers, for here the Soul is apt to emphasize what the Hindus call "The great Sin of Separateness." Also here many become so enwrapped in their own intellectuality, that selfishness is engendered. Hence even if they live in this mental heaven for ages, there must come a time of awakening and realization of their own limitation in heart development, which awakens the desire to advance. The result of this desire in many cases is that they willingly send their consciousness down to the higher regions of the Desire Realm and there learn unselfishness by helping others through inspiring their thoughts with higher ideals; for they can only develop the heart nature by unselfishly working for others.

In this Realm the Soul completes the working out

and perfecting of his mental conceptions, and the plans begun while on earth and continued while in the lower Realms; for here the Soul is in so much closer touch with the ideals in the Mental World that it can grasp greater conceptions of perfection for its plans. As a rule every scientist, inventor or idealist who has an ideal or invention to perfect for humanity, on passing into the astral finds his project awaiting him in as advanced a stage of perfection as he has been able to create. In the lower Realms he continues to work at, enjoy, test and perfect it, but on his dying to those Realms his invention being then freed from the attraction which brought the idea from the Mental World into manifestation, is drawn into the Vital Realm where it will quickly vanish if it contained no vital germ which the life-force could quicken, or the disintegrating currents will dissolve from it all the mistakes and errors which do not correspond with the ideal. The purified pattern will then ascend into the Mental Realm of the astral where it may be still further perfected by its creator. When so perfected it will then descend into a special region in the lower Realms which might be likened to a museum containing all the wonders of the past and those that are to manifest in the future. There it awaits until some mind responds to the idea it embodies, and gives it physical expression. If it is not perfected, it slowly disintegrates and its germ of truth is indrawn into its ideal in the Mental World. It is here, therefore, that the purified thought-forms of inventions, the creations of art, scientific discoveries, etc., are perfected after their purification from flaws and misconceptions in the Vital Realm.

It is here also that the great schools of learning are located, the branches of which we encountered in the lower Realms. Such branches might be compared to the branches of a great university which are located in the slums of a large city and called "Settlement Houses," where university graduates go to live for a time to teach, inspire and uplift the less enlightened of those districts. These great schools are located in this Realm because, being free from the denser astral body and its earth desires, the Soul is able to respond with less effort to the mental environment and give all its attention to intellectual and philosophic pursuits and problems. For here, unhampered by any of the less responsive conditions of the Physical World or of the lower Realms, the mind can easily and quickly grasp and comprehend ideas which only the more advanced Souls, with highly developed and sensitive physical brains, could grasp either while on earth or in the lower Realms. Here it is then that spiritual *ideals* are embodied into definite *ideas* and are so impressed upon the consciousness of the Soul that in its next incarnation they become important factors in the life, even though the physical brain in that incarnation be not sufficiently sensitive and trained to grasp them consciously and fully.

Here it is also that persons who have begun the study of the spiritual philosophy of the Wisdom Religion—and indeed any branch of study or form of religion—continue the more advanced phases of their studies, so that in the next incarnation, the new conceptions are so strongly impressed upon their consciousness that they are born with the conviction of certain truths—such as reincarnation, the persistence of the individual consciousness after so-called death, the possibility of spiritualizing the physical body, etc.—and hence only need to have the attention of their outer consciousness called to such facts to *know* their truth without argument. Of course such convictions also result from study and advance made before leaving the physical body, but they are greatly strengthened by further study in this Mental Realm of the astral after passing on. Therefore our friends the Spiritualists are quite correct in teaching that the friends who have passed beyond the Physical World and beyond the lower Realms of the astral are "still progressing."

In this Realm the schools of philosophy, religion and other branches of learning are quite as various as on earth, and there are many brotherhoods which maintain elaborate organizations for presenting to humanity their conceptions of truth and the principles which they think will be most helpful to mankind. As the race is now entering upon a reincarnation of the period during which the civilization of Atlantis reached its greatest height, the schools of Atlantean philosophy are especially active at this time. Indeed, many famous Atlantean teachers have been waiting all this time to incarnate or represent their perfected teachings to mankind, not having found the dense conditions of previous ages favorable for presenting their advanced teachings or perhaps affording opportunities for more than minor incarnations. Many of these teachers, however, are not even trying to incarnate in this transitional period of the world, but are preparing for a subsequent incarnation by giving out as much of their teachings as possible in advance, through some developed psychic or even through subjective mediums. For while such teachers may not be able to appear in a séance room they can send down their strong thought-currents with such force as to impose them upon subjective mediums and psychics. Such Psychics in turn give out the teachings colored, limited and modified by their stage of intellectual development, personal opinions and preconceived ideas. In such cases there is often an astral entity who first catches the current of thought and then impersonates the Atlantean teacher to the medium. This is also why we have so many books and teachings today which claim to be inspired by or given out by old Atlanteans. In many cases these teachings are but a repetition of the fallacies, sophistries and in some cases the pernicious teachings whose logical development resulted in the downfall of the great Atlantean civilization and the submergence of the continent.

Therefore it is most important that students cultivate their discrimination and intuition and carefully
scrutinize the principles of *any* and *every* teaching
from any source, no matter how apparently high,
and carefully consider how its logical working out
in actual practice will affect humanity. A teaching
should not be accepted merely because it is labeled,
"Atlantean," "psychic," or "spiritual," or because it
comes "from the unseen." The mere label is not sufficient to warrant acceptance, for, as we have seen
above, all kinds of teachings, good, bad and indif-
ferent, from the highest inspiration from the Divine
World and the Masters of Wisdom down to the
platitudes of disembodied orthodox ministers and
the selfish and misleading doctrines of the Brothers
of the Shadow, on down to the lowest and most
pernicious teachings of the Black Brotherhood, all
may come from the so-called "Higher Worlds." And
those who give out such teachings may be innocent agents who are quite sincere in thinking that
their source of information is the highest possible,
merely because it comes from out the invisible.
Discrimination and *intuitive heart-recognition of
Truth*, together with a clear understanding of the
fundamental doctrines of the Wisdom Religion and
the laws of the higher Realms, must therefore be
the watchwords in regard to any and all teachings
claiming to be spiritual.

While the Soul gains and perfects experience
in all Realms of the Astral World, it is principally
because these great Schools of Learning are in the

Mental Realm that the Astral World is called the "Hall of Learning." As we have said elsewhere: "The experiences of the Astral World therefore form part of the training through which every Soul must pass at a certain stage of development ere it can master the problems of the Hall of Learning, be entrusted to function alone and enter the Hall of Wisdom. Although many warnings have been given against entering this World *unprepared*, nevertheless every Soul must pass through its experiences and learn its lessons. The warnings are not so much against entering this World as against lingering amidst its subtle perfumes and wondrous flowers or being misled by the seductive voices or other allurements and fascinations it presents to the inner senses. . . . The Astral World then, is not a region wherein the pupil should seek to dwell and make his home, but merely a country through which he must pass to gain certain necessary Soul-qualities."[1] Therefore, there is no "escaping the astral" as some schools teach. What they really mean is that a long stay in the lower Realms can be escaped and progress greatly advanced by purifying the thoughts, desires and life while still on earth; for as we have already said, it is the four lower and dense Realms that are usually referred to as "the astral."

The only way really to "escape the astral" is so to develop that we can learn most of its lessons while still in physical incarnation. By following the true

---

[1] See lesson *The Great Book*, Part I.

spiritual philosophy and under the guidance of a personal Teacher appointed by the Lodge, after we have reached a certain stage of spiritual growth, the main lessons of the Hall of Learning may be acquired and the Hall of Wisdom of the Mental World entered while still functioning in the flesh, although the higher phases of astral life will have to be experienced for a time after leaving the physical. In the Mental Realm of the Mental World each school of philosophy and religion, etc., is represented by a great mass of mind stuff which differs from all others in density and luminosity "as one star differeth from another in glory." These masses of mind stuff, impregnated with the characteristic ideas of the school formulating them, can be appropriated by anyone capable of reaching up to that Realm of the Mental World. And it is through the Mental Realm of the Astral World that most of the advanced teachers reach up and take as much as they can grasp, develop it and pass it on down to their followers in the Physical World. Occasionally here and there there is an especially advanced Soul who can reach directly into the higher Realms of the Mental World and bring down the teachings to which it affinitizes while still in the physical body; but such instances are comparatively rare, as they are the result of long special training and development through many incarnations.

Chief in importance of all the schools in this Realm of the Astral is the great School of The Lodge

which is maintained and directed by the Masters
of Wisdom of the Great White Lodge for the
promulgation of the Wisdom Religion. Here the
Great Souls who are directly connected with and
immediately supervise the spiritual work in the
Astral and Physical Worlds do their chief work.
These are Great Souls who have won Mastery in
their various Races, but still retain a purified and
spiritualized psychic body that they may easily
keep in touch with the great mass of workers in
the Physical World who, while advanced, intuitive
and spiritual minded, are not able to reach up
directly into the higher and formless Realms and
personally grasp the Divine Wisdom in its more
abstract state and formulate it for themselves.
While many of the more advanced Masters attain
a spiritual Nirmanakaya body, still, most of the
Masters directly connected with the work in the
Physical World, for the sake of helping humanity
the better, voluntarily retain the psychic body.
Hence they retain all the individual characteristics
of the personality and race in which they won
Mastery and so can easily be recognized by those
who knew them when on earth or who are familiar
with their pictures.

The Great White Lodge[2] is composed of those
Great Masters who have attained Mastery through
every school of philosophy and religion, and from
every race of mankind; for Mastery is reaching per-

---

[2] See *Letters from the Teacher*, Curtiss, Chapter II.

fection where all truth is seen as one. This is why it is called the Great White Lodge, for truth is like a diamond which while it reflects every ray of the color spectrum, is nevertheless in itself pure white. So this Great Lodge contains in it the best and the truest from all teachings, and has in it Masters from all schools. Therefore every Soul seeking Mastery over the flesh can find among these Great Souls some Teacher who belongs to the same Hierarchy as himself, *i.e.,* who had the same mental traits and tendencies and has met on the Path the same difficulties, hence can meet that student on his own mental platform, understanding perfectly his difficulties and temptations and thus the more readily give him personal help.

It is in this great School of The Lodge that the Great Teacher known as Mme. Blavatsky, to whom was given the task of preparing the Western World for the coming of the Avatar of the new sub-race, still directs and carries on that great work as one of the most able lieutenants or assistant professors to the Masters who were her Teachers. It is not as the old human personality of Mme. Blavatsky, however, that that Great Teacher should be thought of by her followers, but as the Great Soul who for a time inhabited and was hampered and limited by the traits and frailties of that complex personality. Indeed it is far more in accord with the facts of the case to drop the feminine pronoun entirely and simply refer to that Great Soul as the Teacher, instead of imposing upon her the limitations of the last incarnation in a feminine organism.

The important fact to remember in this connection is that this Great Teacher still remains in the higher Realms of the Astral and from there inspires, works with and influences, *to the degree that each will permit*, respond and follow, not only the Society which she founded and all the sects into which it is now split up, but also every group of students throughout the world who are seeking to promulgate any phase or aspect of the Wisdom Religion and who are unprejudiced and open minded enough to respond to the more advanced conceptions of it to which she has now attained. For remember that even that Great Teacher has advanced far beyond anything which could be grasped while still in the flesh, and has cast off with the limitation of the personality, many of the limiting conceptions of truth held while in the flesh and hence must present new aspects and points of view which were not appreciated or perhaps were unknown while on earth. For it is unthinkable that so great a Soul with so great a mission would lay it aside or cease to advance merely because a hampering overcoat or outer garment of flesh had been laid aside. We can, therefore, say from *positive personal knowledge* and with *special authorization* that this Great Teacher has not incarnated again, as has been frequently reported, and has no intention of doing so again in this Race or even in this World period. For to do so would involve the loss of at least twenty or twenty-five years of precious time during the most vital period of this transitional cycle of the Race, while the new brain and the personality of the new body was being trained as a fitting instrument. Incarnation would also limit the activities of that Teacher to a single human personality, whereas by remaining in the higher Realms of the astral the activities are unlimited and can be carried on with an hundred groups of followers as well as with one, each emphasizing some special phase of the Great Work that might not appeal to the other groups and working with people who would not be attracted to the higher life through any other channel. This is another great reason why all schools, societies and workers in this field, while maintaining their own point of view and doing their own work with their own followers, should nevertheless work more closely hand in hand with their fellow workers than heretofore, thus demonstrating that the Brotherhood they all preach is a *realizable fact among themselves*. Thus they can appear before the world as "Pupils of the same Great Teacher, children of the one sweet mother."

The above explains why this Great Teacher appears to many students in a mist of beautiful, clear, rich violet light; for violet is the color of the higher Realms of the Astral World.

CHAPTER XVI

INDEPENDENT METHODS OF COMMUNION

"Abraham saith unto him, They have Moses and the prophets; let them hear them. And he said, Nay, Father Abraham; but if one went unto them from the dead, they will repent. And he said unto him, If they hear not Moses and the prophets, neither will they be persuaded, though one rose from the dead."

St. Luke, xvi, 29-31

If death is not extinction; then on the other side of dissolution mental activity must continue, and must be interacting with other mental activity."

Raymond, Lodge, 313.

IT is in or through the Mental Realm of the Astral World that we should strive to contact our departed loved ones; for communication with those who have left the Physical World is not only possible— as is now almost universally accepted by scientists who are at all posted as to the investigations of the Society for Psychical Research, to say nothing of the testimony and evidence presented by all the Great Teachers, occultists and mystics throughout the ages—but such communication is perfectly legitimate when conducted according to the laws of *the independent method*. It is quite erroneous to think that our friends pass on so quickly and become so engrossed in their own affairs that they pay little attention to those left behind. The fact is that they remain in touch with us and are often as interested now in our affairs as before passing on; indeed, they are usually more so than before for they can now come much closer to us, understand our thoughts and read our hearts in a way that is impossible, while inhabitating and limited by the physical body, and requiring the clumsy and often misleading methods of speech or writing to express their ideas and desires.

Hence it is just as heartless and cruel, to say nothing of being impolite, to refuse to recognize their presence when felt and to drive them away, as it would be to shut the door in their faces when they came to see us while in the Physical World. Even the more spiritually advanced do not leave their friends and loved ones selfishly to pursue their own spiritual development. Many of them enter the great Schools of The Lodge and work consciously in some capacity to help spread the teachings in both the Astral and Physical Worlds, being especially concerned of course in giving all possible love, help and comfort to those near and dear to them. No Soul who has once vowed allegiance to The Lodge and offered his or her life to its service but will give not one but many lives to its work, until they have attained Mastery and the race has been spiritualized and redeemed.

To turn away from and refuse to recognize our departed loved ones is usually the result of a fear of the astral inculcated by those teachers who, having had little practical training or experience in *properly* contacting the Astral World, know nothing but its dangers. The dangers are terrible and very real, as we have explained in detail in previous chapters, and we have no desire to minimize them in the least. But those who have comprehended what we have written thus far should have conquered all fear and should and can learn perfectly how to protect themselves from the undesirable influences. To such, contacting the Astral World should be no more dangerous than crossing a busy city street or passing saloons, dance-halls, brothels, etc. The dangers are all there in every city and are very real, but no one is obliged to enter a saloon or brothel who does not desire to do so. Just so in the Astral World. Just as on earth, you will be drawn to that with which you affinitize and desire. Hence, if the desires are kept normal and the thoughts pure, and when surrounded by the protecting power of The Christ-light, as we shall explain in detail, there need be no danger.

As we have already said, the departed ones who have reached the Mental Realm can communicate with us only mentally, and those in the lower Realms of the astral should be taught how to communicate only through the Independent or Constructive Method.

There are several natural branches of the Independent Method, all of which are normal and natural avenues of consciousness, although all belong to stages of evolution beyond the average stage of humanity today. Any method of communication is classed as belonging to the Independent Method which does not involve control of any kind; that is, going into a trance or permitting any other consciousness to control either your body—even your hand to write—your mind or your words. At all times you must be fully conscious of what you are saying or doing and use your own discrimination as to whether or not you are willing to stand back of your words and acts. For we are always responsible for our words and acts, whether they are the result of control or not, and we must choose what we say and do. Therefore the Independent Method is one in which the person retains full consciousness of the Physical World and what is going on around him. Retaining full control of all his senses and mental faculties, he is able to judge of what he experiences and is free to react to those experiences as he may choose. The chief among these methods are telepathy, clairvoyance, clairaudience, clairsentience, inspiration, intuition, theophany and avesha. Each of these demands a book for its proper explanation, but here each can only receive the briefest mention, scarcely more than a definition. For further information see special books on each subject.

Telepathy is the direct exchange of consciousness and ideas between mind and mind without any physical means of expression such as speech, writing, etc. According to the author who originated the word, telepathy is "the communication of impressions of any kind from one mind to another, independently of the recognized channels of sense."[1] This is true thought transference or mind reading. This transfer may take place between two or more persons, both of whom are in the flesh or both in the astral, and *also where one is in the astral and one in the flesh*. It is a perfectly safe method because the one receiving the thought of the other can judge it and act accordingly.

Clairvoyance is simply the development of the ability to see in the Astral World as well as in the Physical. Those who are clairvoyant (clear-visioned) can also see reflected in the Astral that which is transpiring in the Physical World, no matter what the distance. Such persons can also see the symbolic visions projected either by the Higher Self or by the Masters of Wisdom for their instruction, warning or guidance. They can also see the events and thoughts pictured in the aura of a mortal, hence the vogue of clairvoyant "readings." But since the aura of a person is sacred and given each one that

---

[1] *Human Personality*, Myers, I, xxii.

perfect privacy may be enjoyed, it is just as rude and uncouth to enter the aura of a person unasked as it would be to enter the private chamber unasked of one who forgot to lock the door. A Master or refined spiritual helper will always knock at the door and ask permission to enter. Hence do not wonder why the Masters do not read your every thought; you might be sorry if They did—you must invite Them.

As the proper interpretation of what is seen is all important, a "reading" by an ignorant and untrained clairvoyant is of little value; indeed, it may be distinctly misleading, even pernicious, especially, if it is accepted as certain truth and unalterable fate. Clairvoyance, therefore, is to be used and accepted only subject to your best judgment.

Clairaudience is the ability to hear what is transpiring in the astral or at a distance on earth. The clairaudient (clear-hearing) cannot only hear the voices of departed friends, but also nature sounds, elementals, etc. It is legitimate but must also be subject to good judgment. In fact it cannot be too greatly emphasized that in all advanced spiritual development it is most important to cultivate discrimination, good judgment and common sense.

Clairsentience is the power of grasping the reality and truth of things through mere contact. This also includes psychometry. Through this faculty you sense the truth of what you hear, see or feel. It can also be used on earth to sense conditions and states of consciousness around you. On entering a room for instance a clairsentient person will know the character of conversation or thought that has been held up to the time he entered or that may have been carried on in it years ago. A phase of this faculty manifests as the homing instinct, whether in birds, animals or men. A person who has this faculty knows what another is going to say almost as soon as, or even before, the first word is spoken, and often knows better than the speaker how it should be expressed. Hence such persons have an almost uncontrollable desire to correct the speaker and are very inattentive and poor listeners. In this phase it overlaps intuition, yet we make a distinction. The danger of this faculty is that the one using it may let personal bias enter into its use, thus making good judgment difficult.

Intuition is Soul guidance or tuition from within, from your own Father-in-Heaven. It differs from clairsentience in that in the latter we merely sense the thing, while in intuition our own Divine Higher Self has impressed it upon our consciousness or taught it to us. It also manifests as conscience which discriminates between right and wrong. It is the faculty above all others necessary in dealing with all phases of the Astral World.

Inspiration is the breathing into your consciousness of the Spirit. When inspired by a scene or by music the Spirit of that scene or music enters into you and reveals to your consciousness its real significance or Soul. You can also be inspired by an astral friend, a Spiritual Teacher, by a Divine Being or by abstract ideals. The degree of your inspiration depends upon how perfectly your mentality can express it. You can be inspired from any Realm or World either to paint, sing, speak, write or any other form of expression. But you must use your own judgment, first as to where the inspiration comes from, and second whether or not you desire to respond to it. This must not be confused with astral control. In the astral control you are a mere puppet or tool, having little or no control over what is said or written or done, even no knowledge of it, while in inspiration you are a conscious messenger of a higher power. Inspiration overlaps telepathy in those cases in which the inspiration comes from some person or Teacher by means of telepathy, but is direct when the consciousness reaches directly to the realities, spiritual verities and ideals in the higher Realms or Worlds which you desire to represent.

Theophany is "the direct manifestation of the gods (or Spiritual Teachers) to man by actual appearance." This appearance can be manifested only to a specially trained mortal. Theophany could, therefore come only from a Divine source, never from an astral entity. This is the method by which most of the scriptures of the world, including the Christian, have been transmitted to man. For instance, the Spiritual Teacher appeared to the spiritual vision of St. John and *said*: "What thou seest, write in a book." What was written was not written under "control" or through "automatic writing," but *independently*, while the transcriber was in full working consciousness. There are many other references to this Independent Method in the Bible, showing that it was the method universally used to give spiritual teachings to mankind.

"The surest means of obtaining knowledge of the gods, and of their will, was through their direct personal manifestation in visible theophanies."[2] But there is the chance of some astral entity calling himself such a Divine Being and seeking to impress teachings on the unwary, hence you must always demand in the name of The Living Christ who it is, as was done by all inspired writers; for we read of their challenging in the words, "Who art thou Lord?" so often repeated in the scriptures.

Avesha is a peculiar relation between a chosen mortal—trained and perfected for this special relation through many incarnations—and a Divine Being or a more than mortal Spiritual Teacher, for the purpose of presenting to the world a particular truth, message or philosophy. This latter method sums up and includes the other seven methods of Independent Communion, for a true Avesha has all the above faculties developed. There can be no deception here, for by their works are they known.

All the above mentioned methods of communica-

---

[2] *Beginnings of Christianity*, Fisher, 84.

tion require special conditions and special training for their development, either in this life or in the past, theophany and avesha requiring training of the most advanced and spiritual character through many incarnations devoted almost entirely to the spiritual life and its requirements. Among these methods telepathy is the one which requires the least training and which can most quickly be developed by the average seeker. It is therefore the one we advocate as the most practical and satisfactory for those who are not born with some of their astral senses already partially opened.

All these methods are classed as *constructive* because they all result from the *normal unfoldment* of the senses of man in the Astral World, and are therefore but a continuation of the constructive processes of life which ever tend toward balance, self-control and perfection. At the risk of being tedious to the many students who have followed our various books and teachings for years, we must repeat in this connection what we have said elsewhere concerning the difference between the Independent or Constructive Method and the Subjective or Destructive Method.[3]

"Still another way in which the doors are frequently broken open is by placing yourself in a passive, non-resisting state and making a demand for psychic experiences, or sitting for development as it is called.

---

[3] *Voice of Isis*, 104-8. Also *Letters from the Teacher*, 55-6.

In this practice you are placing yourself in such a
negative state that any entity dwelling on the lower
astral plane can help you break open the doors. This
either destroys the doors or abnormally forces the
development of the psychic centers instead of
unfolding them as a natural accompaniment of
spiritual growth. When results have been thus
obtained, since the doors are not under the control
of your will, they are open to any entity who desires
to obsess you. Even if the obsessing entity is a
disembodied friend of good moral character, your
condition is not altered, for he must be near you
constantly to protect you from fiends.[4] This is what
takes place in ordinary subjective mediumship."

As we said in *Letters from the Teacher,*[5] "The
difference between spiritual communication and
subjective mediumship is a difference both of vibration and method. The right way to contact the
higher planes is to raise the vibrations of your
physical and psychic bodies and their centers until
they vibrate in harmony with the keynote of the
Soul plane, at which pitch 'no evil thing can come
nigh thy dwelling.' As we can only become aware
of a thing when some part of our organism responds
to its vibrations, the psychic must have the proper
development to come into harmony with the spiritual plane ere he can contact the Masters or respond
to things which touch upon or vibrate within the
octave of their keynote.

---

[4] See *The Shadow Land*, by Hamlin Garland.
[5] Page 118, 3rd edition.

"On the one hand—spiritual communication—the psychic, through spiritual living, loving
thoughts and helpful actions in many lives, must
build into his or her character enough of the divine
principle of Compassion for all humanity to raise
the vibrations of all the bodies, either temporarily or continuously, to the note of spiritual love to
which the Masters of Compassion naturally vibrate.
On the other hand—subjective mediumship—the
psychic, through various means, either mentally
by stilling the thoughts, or physically by various
yoga practices such as gazing at a crystal, a black
spot, or sitting in a constrained position, through
breathing exercises and many other still more
objectionable practices—has gained the power
of stilling the physical vibrations and becoming
negative; or when through the oily sheaths having
become weakened or destroyed the psychic is naturally negative. In such a state the physical atoms,
not being held together by the vibratory rhythm
to which they naturally respond, slow down and
fly off to such an extent that any discarnate entity,
clothed in atoms of, and vibrating to the note of,
the astral plane, which is next to and in its lower
degrees overlaps the earth plane, can gather up and
clothe himself in sufficient of the physical atoms
thus thrown off to temporarily vibrate to the keynote of the physical plane and become temporarily
recognizable on that plane.

"In the first instance, the whole desire of the
psychic is to uplift humanity; he is filled with Com-

passion for the race and desires to give himself as
a willing sacrifice to bring enlightenment to the
world. This is the true spiritual development. The
Teachers and Masters whom he contacts do not see
the little individual difficulties, or if They do, They
understand the Law and know that all is working
out for the best, that only wisdom can really help.
Given Wisdom, Love and sustaining help, the
disciples can, and indeed must work out their own
personal problems. As Paul says: 'Work out your
own salvation with fear and trembling.' All spiritual
communication is uplifting, and the spiritual atoms
which the psychic has contacted and drawn into his
body will rejuvenate and strengthen the physical,
uplift the mental and advance him on the Path of
Spiritual Attainment.

"In the second instance, by giving up the command over the life-forces and throwing open or
breaking down the doors of the sacred centers, the
vitality is drawn upon and the atoms thrown off are
used to bring to the physical plane the denizens of the
astral.[6] These may be pure or vile, and are attracted
to the medium in exact ratio to the state of the atoms
which he or she gives off during the negative 'sitting.' If you understand this, and the fact that most
of the entities contacted upon the astral plane are not
Spiritual Beings, but merely men and women with
their most dense and outer garment (the physical

---

[6] See *Letters from a Living Dead Man*, Barker, 34, 54.

body) removed, you will understand the danger of giving yourself to their use. They can only come to earth as they left it, *i.e.,* clothed in physical atoms; the fact that to manifest on the physical plane they must steal physical atoms from the medium and sitters is proof positive of this. The first is the *Constructive*, the second the *Destructive* method of communication. In no case—unless they are Masters, in which case they will manifest quite differently, as we will explain later—are they different from the people on earth, except that they are functioning in a body composed of finer matter.

"You cannot always tell which of the above mentioned methods have been used by the teachings received, for even in subjective mediumship the teaching may be of a higher moral character, just as some friend might give you a highly moral address. But no matter who the entity claims to be, he will not be a Master of Wisdom if the subjective method is used, for no Master of the Right Hand Path ever uses that method. In this case it is not a question of what teachings are given, but how they are given. . . . "One absolute test as to which method a psychic is using and from whence the messages come is the effect on the physical body. In spiritual communication the psychic is clothed upon by spiritual atoms which self-effacement and compassion have drawn to him, and he grows more spiritual. If after the experience his vitality is augmented, and a peaceful, happy and vigorous feeling remains, even for days afterward; if life seems fuller, trials easier to bear and love more abundant, you can rest assured that he has risen above earthly things and has been clothed upon by the Spirit, and has brought back lessons for the benefit of humanity. This is the form of communion with the higher planes that should be desired. But do not strive for it; let it come as a natural growth resulting from a life filled with loving, unselfish thoughts and deeds.

"In subjective mediumship, however, owing to the loss of physical atoms and vitality, the psychic is depleted and weakened, and soon shows it, not only in bodily health, but also in mental power. His nervous system is enervated his mentality is dulled and a great stumbling block has been placed in his path. If, after communicating, the psychic is exhausted, tired, nervous, cross, fretful, and uneasy, even for days, you can rest assured that he has allowed some astral entity to absorb his vitality and contact him by the second and destructive method."

"The student can quickly tell whether he has contacted an advanced Spiritual Teacher or merely a disembodied mortal, by the feeling which results, even if his intuition does not reveal it to him. When the Spiritual Teachers are contacted the spiritual force of their auras will be felt like a fire, so that instead of the chill felt on contacting an astral entity a wave of warmth, life and vitality will seem to well up from within and surround him. This warmth.

is often so great as to make the body break out in
perspiration and the wave of love-force is so great
that the throat chokes with emotion and the eyes
fill with tears of joy. This physical reaction is really
a protection to the centers in the physical body;
for both Divine Love and Divine Life are aspects
of fire, and if the love-nature is not sufficiently
purified and developed to withstand so great an
influx of Divine Fire its centers might be greatly
damaged if a physical reaction was possible.

"You would hesitate to lend your body to any
of your friends on earth to do with as they pleased
and the mere passing over makes no difference
whatever; they are able to use their astral faculties which are a little finer than the physical, but
that is all. They are just as spiritually advanced as
when on earth, know just as much of the laws of
life, but no more. Never give them any form of
worship. Simply take such advice as they have to
give as you would take their advice when upon
earth, *i.e.,* subject to your own good judgment and
common-sense."

All these advanced steps bring with them their
own dangers and temptations. For no matter how
high we climb we can always fall until we, like
Jesus, become one with the Father. Yet we can conquer every temptation and forestall every danger if
we live in the Divine Consciousness of the One Life
and walk humbly hand in hand with The Christ and
not let ambition overwhelm us.

CHAPTER XVII

SUBJECTIVE METHODS

'At first I took only your arm to write with. . . .
yet I could not do it long at a time without using
your own vitality."
Letters from a Living Dead Man, Barker, 34-54.

"It may be well to give a word of warning to those
who find that they possess any unusual power in
the psychic direction. . . . self-control is more
important than any other form of control. . . .
To give up your own judgment and depend solely
on adventitious aid is a grave blunder, and may in
the long run have disastrous consequences."
Raymond, Lodge, 225.

ALTHOUGH the authors are not spiritualists
and this is not a work on spiritualism, it is deemed
advisable that the chief subjective methods of communication with the Astral World receive brief
mention.

Under subjective methods we class all those
methods which *subject the consciousness, mind or
body to the control of the will of another*, especially
those methods which cause the ones so controlled to
be unconscious of what is being said or done through
them. It is also a subjective method in which such

persons know what is taking place but are powerless to prevent or even alter the procedures, because they have given over the control to another intelligence, either disembodied or embodied (as in hypnosis).

While it is true that many worthy persons practice subjective methods who in themselves are honest, earnest, sincere and pure, and much helpful and comforting information may be transmitted through such methods, nevertheless we deplore and strongly discourage the use of such methods for three main reasons, although there are others. Remember we do not deny either the honesty of the medium—although there are many frauds as we shall explain later on—or the correctness of the communication, but we object to the *method* used.

In the first place, putting one's body under the control of another makes such an one an irresponsible puppet, a mere tool to work the will of another and without the power to prevent the most outrageous lies from being told or to decide whether the actions performed or the teachings given by such a control are desirable or not. Such control, instead of expanding the consciousness and developing the intellect and heart qualities of the medium, stultifies mental growth and makes him dependent on his controls or "guides" for understanding and direction, instead of upon his own judgment and the guidance of his own Divine Soul within. This same objection applies to those who continually seek guidance from their departed loved ones. Instead of using judgment and common-sense and learning the lessons which life here in the Physical World is meant to teach them, praying for enlightenment and guidance from within when help is needed, such persons rush to the nearest medium and seek advice from their astral friends. This also takes away initiative, undermines judgment and makes the recipient more or less of a puppet, acting not according to his own rational processes, but on the mere dictum of another, an essentially irrational process.

In dealing with our departed friends, we should clearly remember, as we explain in *Letters from the Teacher*,[1] that they are not angels or spiritual beings, nor have they suddenly become endowed with wisdom. They are merely men and women with their most dense outer garment or overcoat (the physical body) removed. "Since they are using their astral senses they can see farther ahead than those on the earth plane, but such advice as they have to give should be taken just as you would take their advice while on earth—subject to your own good judgment and common-sense. Often their desire is to help alleviate earthly conditions, but their advice, while valuable in many cases, is still largely in accord with worldly standards. In fact their activity is often like that of a well meaning but over-meddlesome friend on the earth plane. In no

---

[1] Page 55, 3rd edition.

case are they different from the people of earth
except that they are functioning in a body composed
of finer matter." They have the same desires, habits,
modes of thought, tastes, prejudices and friendships
that they had before taking off the garment of
flesh. In fact their personality is no more altered
than is our personality different when we remove
a hampering overcoat, except for such changes
as may be due to their progress after leaving the
Physical World. Therefore a knowledge of the
laws of the Astral World, together with common
sense, balance, poise and purity of thought are most
important for one who attempts to communicate
with the Astral World.

In the second place, the *process* of control is
essentially a degenerating one. In a normal and independent contact with the Higher Worlds all the
currents of magnetism, astral currents and even of
consciousness itself, are flowing in the direction of
normal evolution and unfoldment, *i.e.*, outward and
upward, from lower worlds to higher, from lower
rates of vibration to higher. But in the effort to bring
a disembodied entity down from a higher world,
from the higher octave of vibration of the Astral
World down to the lower octave of the Physical
World, as is necessary to control the body of the
medium, all the normal currents are *reversed*. The
centers by which the medium contacts the astral,
instead of being opened from within outward as
in normal development, are now *forced open* from

without inward. And the result is similar to that which occurs when a door is forced open the wrong way, *i.e.*, its fastenings are broken and it swings idly on its hinges, easily pushed open by any passerby. Therefore just as the upward and outward flowing currents are constructive and upbuilding, so their reversal is necessarily destructive and disintegrating. The proof of this is plainly evident in the depleted condition that so universally follows the use of these methods, a condition testified to by all investigators in psychic research.

In the third place, the subjective method has a similarly degenerative effect upon the entities thus drawn down from their place in the astral into the dense earth magnetism, earth conditions, and into the earthly body of the medium. This effect is also testified to by many investigators, as for instance *Raymond*, referring to the difficulties found in controlling a medium says: "He (the astral control) wanted to speak through her, but he found it very difficult. . . . He started. . . . and then he didn't feel like himself. . . . what worries him is that *he didn't feel like himself*."[2]

Furthermore, such control is a *temporary obsession*, which frequently becomes more or less permanent. The suffering and torture, the anguish and despair which mediums undergo under such conditions is fully described and substantiated by Dr. J. M.

---

[2] *Raymond*, Lodge, 241.

Peebles—himself a veteran spiritualist well known in spiritualistic circles around the world in his book on *Spirit Obsessions*.

Full subjective control is usually preceded by a transitional state called trance, and the two terms control and trance are often used without distinction. There are several other forms of trance however. Two should be distinguished here as not being subjective but independent. One is where the sensitive person simply leaves the body in a state of passivity or partially suspended animation, while he or she ascends into the Higher Worlds in search of the information desired. As long as the body or consciousness is not controlled by another, but the body is simply left tenantless, this is not a destructive process.

A second form of independent trance is that experienced in true ecstasy. In this condition the Soul has entered into Realms of light and glory where the states of consciousness are so spiritual and exalted that the body and its consciousness is transcended and hence remains apparently lifeless. On the return to normal consciousness after these flights, far from being enervated and depleted by the experience, the sensitive is filled with life and energy, joy and happiness, for he has brought back with him something of the glory and spiritual life-force he experienced in the higher Realms or Worlds. This latter is the condition so frequently referred to in the *Bible* as being "caught up in the spirit." When St. John was "in the spirit on the Lord's day" he was not under control, nor was *Revelation* given through automatic writing of any kind. He was simply in an ecstatic condition during which the Lord (or Spiritual Teacher) told him what to write, and he wrote it while in full possession of all his faculties, able to refuse if he wished.

The phenomenon of materialisation is the most depleting and degenerating of all. In this procedure, the medium goes into a dead trance and allows his physical counterpart[3] to be withdrawn and moulded into the likeness of the departed one who desires to manifest. In the case of the English medium, Mr. Elington it is reported that "his dense body shrivelled perceptibly; and that the same phenomena has been observed with Mr. Husk, whose dense body became too reduced to fill out his clothes. Mr. Elington's body once was so diminished in size that a *materialized* form carried it out and presented it for inspection to the sitters—one of the few cases in which both medium and materialized form have been visible together in light sufficient to allow of examination." This method requires so much vitality from the sitters and is so degenerating to the medium that it cannot be too strongly condemned, as it invariably has been in all scriptures and by all great Spiritual Teachers.

Another form of communication must be mentioned here as it is usually conducted in a subjective way; that is with the medium either under control or in a dead trance—*i.e.*, one in which the astral

---

[3] The material of which, when extruded from the physical like a vapor and then condensed into a cold, jelly-like mass is now called "ectoplasm."

body is withdrawn for the purpose of performing the phenomena—but is sometimes conducted in an independent method, namely trumpet speaking. In this procedure—usually conducted in the dark, but rarely in the light—through the peculiar development of the medium the departed ones are given sufficient physical magnetism and astral force to enable them to speak audibly through a trumpet or megaphone. This is perhaps the most satisfactory form of message from the lower Realms of the Astral World, for in an honest and properly conducted trumpet séance the seeker can recognize and positively identify the voice and manner of speaking of the departed one. Where this method is used *without the medium going under control or into a trance* it is legitimate, although not advisable to repeat at frequent intervals; for a certain amount of magnetism, life-force and physical atoms must be drawn from the sitters to reinforce that of the medium to secure satisfactory physical results.

Under the head of subjective and destructive methods we must also include the Ouija board, planchette and automatic writing, painting, etc., for they are all forms of more or less partial, and are easily developed into complete, control. That those who are not familiar with it may recognize it, the Ouija board may be described as a small lap-board, such as is sometimes used by ladies when sewing, on which the letters of the alphabet are arranged in a semicircle along the farther side, with the words "yes" and "no" in the two further corners. A small three-legged table about the size of the hand accompanies the board. The board is placed either upon the lap or upon a table and those who are to operate it lightly place the tips of their fingers upon the little three-legged table. Questions are then asked of the invisible entities in the astral. These are answered by those entities controlling the hands of the ones touching the little table to such an extent that it is pushed along the board from letter to letter until it spells out the answer to the question. The planchette is a similar arrangement except that in place of one of the legs the little table contains an upright pencil which writes the words instead of spelling them out.

It is quite evident that someone whose fingers touch the little table must be sensitive enough for the astral entity to control his or her arm sufficiently to make the table move in the direction of the letter desired. Manifestly *this is a form or first step in the process of control* by an astral entity, and as the operator has no means of knowing who or what the control is, he or she is throwing open his or her aura and body to the entrance and control of any obsessing elemental, criminal or demon from any Realm who may chance to be passing or who may be attracted by the force displayed and the desires sent out. We have known this method to be the beginning of terrible obsessions and so advise most strongly against its use. Although it is often

possible for well meaning friends to come into
touch with those left behind through these methods,
yet owing to the ease with which impersonation and
fraud can be introduced and the great difficulty of
being sure that the one controlling the board is what
he claims to be, it is extremely dangerous.[4]

Automatic writing is performed by some astral
entity taking control of the hand and arm of some
sensitive person and using it to write a message, the
contents of which may be quite unknown to the person so used. This, of course, is also a form of control,
hence is necessarily depleting, as is testified to by
nearly all who have had any great experience with

---

[4] A case of gross and wilful deception has recently been investigated by the
authors. A student began experimenting with the Ouija board and soon began
getting messages purporting to be from his mother, many convincing personal
incidents and details being given. For months he was told his only sister would
be drowned while on a visit to friends at a summer resort. Upon the advice of
the Ouija board he drew a considerable sum of money from the bank and kept
it in the house, ready for instant use. Summer plans were changed and business
trips cancelled as the fatal day drew near. Finally, in the presence of the authors,
the son was told that his sister had been drowned the previous day and was
now with the mother in the Astral World, also that a message had been sent him
which he failed to get. After two days and nights of the greatest anxiety and
suffering on the part of the son and his wife the sister returned home alive and
well and without having been in a boat or on the water. No message had been
sent, and the communications lasting for months were proved to be the most
wilful deceptions and barefaced frauds.

it,'[5] although if the control understands the law, the depletion may be partially counteracted and many beautiful and interesting messages given, as in the case of *Patience Worth, Letters from a Living Dead Man*, etc.

It is also possible to write inspirationally, but this must be distinguished from automatic writing. In such a case the sensitive will be fully aware of choosing words and expressions. For instance, the inspired thought may come in language so beautiful that the intellect of the one receiving it cannot do it justice, and he may consciously try to express it in more simple terms. In such a case, although it may be inspired by another, it will not be astral control, hence is legitimate.

---

[5] "Even automatic writing has its risks. . . . Even so apparently harmless a method of communication has led to tragedies in the past, and is calculated, if not carefully handled, to lead to similar tragedies in the future. There is a method of hypnotization which seems to be employed by communicating entities which, if not resisted, may well end in the lunatic asylum.—Editorial, *The Occult Review*, London, July, 1917. Also see *Raymond*, Sir Oliver Lodge, 162, 194, 219, and *Letters of a Living Dead Man*, Barker, 54.

CHAPTER XVIII

THE TELEPATHIC METHOD

"Believe not every Spirit, but try the Spirits whether they be of God; because many false prophets are gone into the world."

I John, iv, 1.

"Life and mind and consciousness do not belong to the material region; whatever they are in themselves, they are manifestly something quite distinct from matter and energy, and yet they utilize the material and dominate it."

Raymond, Lodge, 317.

TO develop the telepathic method in the most advantageous way, first repeat some prayer[1] or invocation which will focus The Christ-light in your aura that it may fill and surround you and protect you from all forces which cannot vibrate to its Light, Truth and Purity, such prayers for instance as our *Prayer for Light, the Healing Prayer*, etc.[2] Then picture to yourself the face of the loved one you desire to reach and send that one a mental invitation to come and visit you if at liberty to do so. Be

---

[1] "There's a lot in prayer, prayer keeps out evil things, and keeps nice clean conditions; Raymond says, keeps out devils."   *Raymond*, Lodge, 227.

[2] See Appendix.

careful, however, not to make a picture of the face as it appeared in sickness or in death. Neither should you hold a sorrowful or lugubrious attitude of mind in which you implore the loved ones to come to you because you are so sad and lonely. Instead prepare a glad countenance and a feeling of joyful anticipation, such as you would feel when welcoming them home from a long journey. In short think more of giving and entertaining than of receiving; for cheerful and happy thoughts of love make an atmosphere about you which attracts your friends, while selfish, sad and depressing thoughts make a pall of fog about you which prevents them from seeing you or coming near you. In the beginning you may write a letter to the loved one just as if he were in the flesh. Explain just what you desire to accomplish, then leave the letter open near your bed or under your pillow when you retire and the answer will be impressed upon you.

When a presence is sensed or felt in any way and you become aware of some one near you, the first thing is always to challenge that presence "In the name of The Christ." Later on by holding the determined thought of the protecting power of The Christ and the persistent thought that you will have nothing to do with anything that is not true, pure and helpful, you can so impregnate your aura with this power and this attitude of mind that it becomes a perpetual challenge; for The Christ within will make you intuitively aware of that which is false.

As we have said elsewhere: "The right hand is always a symbol of purity and the power of the light to prevail; it also refers to the positive pole or that which is to manifest in expression, while the left hand is the negative or unmanifested pole. When the left hand is applied to manifested or earth conditions it symbolizes the negative or evil aspect of the manifestation in question. Students whose inner faculties are unfolding and who are beginning to have psychic experiences can easily protect themselves from unpleasant experiences and imposture by remembering this symbology, for no false or evil entity can take its stand upon your right hand in response to your command. The rule is first to determine that you will allow no entity or psychic experience come to you that does not come in love and purity for your best good. Make this determination so strong that it will impress even your subconscious mind—the mind of the animal self—so that your very attitude will be a protection in itself, just as a similar attitude will protect you in the Physical World. When you have a psychic experience which penetrates this protecting aura always challenge it. Learn by heart these words and use them: 'In the name of the Living Christ I demand to know who you are and what your mission is. If you come for my good take your stand on my right hand. Reveal yourself and answer truthfully or in the name of The Christ begone.'

"If the entity tries to evade the challenge or to cajole

you with such words as 'You know me, dear one; you know I would not harm you, so why should you challenge me?' etc., refuse to reply or have anything to do with it. *Permit no argument or excuses*, but insist upon a true answer to your challenge. It is a law upon the psychic plane that no entity can withstand this challenge when The Christ-force is truly invoked; it must either reveal its true nature or disappear. As the *Bible* truly tells us, 'The Lord is a consuming fire' and upon the psychic plane The Christ-force is an actual flame which nothing that does not vibrate to its keynote of truth and purity can resist, no matter how beautiful or glorious it may seem to you. The Masters of Wisdom or Their messengers, also your real friends, will gladly comply with such a challenge. It is the Law, and your challenge proves that you are obeying the law, for you cannot protect yourself from deception in that world of glamor and illusion until you have learned to test all things with the above challenge in one form or another."[3]

That this is no new teaching, but a well-known, although little understood Christian teaching, is shown in what is practically the identical method given us by St. John: "Every spirit that confesseth that Jesus Christ is come in the flesh (that is, who answers The Christ challenge) is of God. And every spirit that confesseth not that Jesus Christ is

---

[3] See lesson, *The Great Book*, Part II.

come in the flesh (*i.e.,* who cannot answer to the challenge) is not of God."[4] When a spirit answers the challenge given in the name of the Living Christ by obeying you, his obedience is the confession that Jesus Christ has come in the flesh, and that the Spirit of Christ is in your flesh. We may also repeat here the quotation at the head of this chapter: "Believe not every spirit, but try the spirits whether they be of God; because many false prophets are gone into the world." Also Paul's injunction: "Prove all things; hold fast to that which is good."

If the presence of the entity which you sense near you brings a cold chill or a disagreeable feeling of any kind you will know that the person contacted is not in the Mental Realm but in one of the lower Realms, and the astral body is abstracting heat and vitality from you, as described on page 83. In such a case tell the person quietly but firmly that he must not come so near you, but *must stand off at a distance*, well outside your aura, and communicate with you *through telepathy*. Otherwise such an entity will unconsciously throw over you its astral conditions and sap your vitality, something which you by no means desire and should not permit. If, on the other hand, the presence contacted brings a thrill of love and a wave of heat, instead of chill and dread, you will know that the contact has not been made with the astral body, but in one of the higher

---

[4] *I John,* iv, 3-4.

Realms or perhaps with one of the higher Teachers. When the right kind of contact is made there will be a wave of certainty and confidence and an intuitive recognition that all is well, and until this confidence is attained the challenge should be continued.

When the presence has answered the challenge in a way that brings the thrill of love and confidence or by some prearranged sign or signal that is satisfactory to you, such as standing on your right hand, etc., speak to it mentally—or even audibly if you are alone where you cannot be overheard and considered demented—and ask the question you desire. While you may not be able to hear a voice or see a form that you can identify, unless you are clairaudient or clairvoyant, the proof that the presence is really the loved one you believe it to be is that the answers to your questions seem to flash into your mind, not in the terms you or some other person would naturally employ in expressing themselves, but in the expressions and with all the little peculiarities of speech which are *character-istic of that particular loved one*. Often while you are busy and thinking of other things, the picture, voice or thought of the loved one will suddenly enter your consciousness in a particularly vivid way. When this occurs at once speak to the one who is thus presented to you and establish communication.

These tests, together with the nature of the replies themselves, will positively identify the speaker and will be most convincing. But if, in spite of your challenging, an imposter should attempt to impersonate your loved one there will always be a feeling of doubt, if not actual distrust and even loathing, which will warn you that all is not as it should be. Such an intuitive warning is always received, provided you are not too excited or flattered by the fact of the communion to give heed to it; for once you have sincerely placed your consciousness and your aura in the keeping and under the protection of The Christ you may trust it to warn you. Therefore in case of such doubts or warnings do not attempt to continue the communication at that time. And the next time it is attempted you should send out a mental call either for the Teacher of this Order, or The Christ, to send you a protecting helper until you are thoroughly trained, as much to train the one desiring to communicate with you as to protect yourself. Also tell your loved ones to ask for the workers of this Order to instruct and help them in whatever Realm they may be. But remember that you must learn to rely upon the power of The Christ-light within yourself for protection and guidance. As long as you rely upon some outside agency, no matter how high, you will remain but a babe in the kindergarten of the higher life.

A special warning must here be given against trying to communicate with a sui-cide, for the peculiar conditions in which a suicide is compelled to dwell—described in a previous chapter—are such that he cannot communicate with you without throwing over

you the same black cloud of depression and the
same insane impulse which impelled him to take his
life. If such an one should be contacted, absolutely
refuse to communicate with him or permit him to
enter your aura. Instead, direct him to call out for
Light and seek for Teachers in the Astral World
who are especially trained in nursing such persons
and who are qualified to give them all possible help
and instruction.

Another special case must also be called to
your attention and guarded against. Frequently a
loved one in the astral will try to gain the attention and come into rapport with a loved one on
earth, especially when the mortal is of the opposite sex, by overshadowing some sensitive mortal
of his own sex to such an extent that for the moment the sensitive might seem to have taken on
the features of the one in the astral. In other cases
the overshadowing one may momentarily pour
out, through the eyes of the sensitive, his love for
the dear one left on earth. In such cases the living person will both see and feel the great wave of
love coming through the overshadowed sensitive,
and unless properly instructed and warned, may
naturally think that the sensitive mortal through
whom the departed one is manifesting is himself
personally in love with (in this case) her, whereas
the sensitive is either entirely unconscious of what
is taking place through him or perhaps feels but
a wave of sympathy or friendly feeling. A number of cases have been called to our attention in
which this has occured and caused unnecessary

jealousies and heartaches, if not disaster, before the real state of the case could be explained; hence this warning.

It is just such phenomena as this which have brought misunderstandings, scandals, ill repute and disaster to many psychics, mediums, sensitives and Spiritual Teachers whose love, sympathy and desire to help have placed them in such a receptive, if not actually negative, state that this form of partial and momentary obsession takes place. This is also one explanation of why so many professional psychics cause so much trouble in family relations. The great lesson to be learned from this is that all students who realize that they are sensitive and in more or less conscious touch with the Astral World should take particular pains never to allow themselves to get into a negative state.

The teachings of many spiritualists is that the pupils should place themselves in as negative a state as possible, for their object is more easily to permit control or obsession by their astral friends. But the teachings of this Order are that all should impregnate their minds and auras with a *positive* mental attitude which will not permit such a partial obsession to manifest through them even for the moment.

These instructions are not given to stimulate mere curiosity and a desire to dabble in astral conditions — for we again remind you of the terrible dangers recounted in previous chapters, to be encountered by those who are not both ready and properly trained for such experiments—but are given to help the hundreds of students who are *already more or less in touch* with astral conditions and who, since their eyes are once opened, must continue in touch with those conditions and learn to function in them, just as a child when once born cannot be thrust back into the womb, but must learn to use its faculties and meet the conditions in which it finds itself. It is therefore most important, instead of merely instilling fear, that the *definite, well-tried and proved rules* be given out, which *when implicitly obeyed* will make communication with the Astral World free from danger. It is dangerous to handle instruments in an electrical laboratory or power-house, but those who are to become electricians must learn to work freely with all such instruments, and this they can do without danger only by implicitly obeying the rules laid down by electrical science. The same principles apply to using the psychic instruments by which you contact the Astral World.

CHAPTER XIX

THE INSPIRATIONAL OR SPIRITUAL REALM

"Every mortal has his immortal counterpart or rather his Archetype, in heaven. This means that the former is indissolubly united to the latter in each of his incarnations, and for the duration of the cycle of births."

The Secret Doctrine, Blavatsky, ii, 59.

"By faith Enoch was translated that he should not see death; and was not found, because God took him; for before his translation he had this testimony, that he pleased God."

Hebrews, xi, 5.

THIS is the Realm of the Astral which corresponds to the Spiritual World and to the Spiritual Soul or Buddhic Principle of man. It is therefore the Realm of the ideal, that region of the astral in which there exist the spiritual prototypes of that which is later embodied in the lower Realms and finally manifested in a limited and more or less imperfect way on earth. It is the spiritual and perfect patterns in this Realm and in the Mental World that are the source of creative inspiration. It is in this Realm that the artist senses the perfect types of form and proportion; where he revels in the wondrous play of exquisite and irridescent hues and shadings of vibrant and living color, compared with which the most vivid pigments of earth, through which they strive to express, seem dull and dead. Hence the disappointment of the inspired artist who tries to reproduce on canvas the beauties his inner vision has glimpsed.

In this Realm also the musician hears the ravishing melodies which thrill his Soul and whose message he strives to express in the strains of his aria, rhapsody or symphony. Here, too, the poet senses those pure, high and divine ideals which he endeavors to express in the rhythm and imagery of his verse. From this source also are derived those high and advanced conceptions which burst into manifestation in the flashes of genius which make for the advancement, help and uplift of mankind or whose misunderstanding or perversion works harm or retards evolution.

This is the region reached in high spiritual dreams and visions, also the region from which glimpses of past lives are gained.

This Realm is the subdivision of the astral in which the Spiritual Beings known as Devas and Kumaras appear when they descend to manifest in the Astral World. It is in this Realm also where dwell those Adepts who have reached the degree of Mastery which we call Christhood. Such Masters, having conquered all earth conditions, no longer need an earthly or physical instrument; in fact, would be greatly hampered by it. Yet their work for humanity is by no means over or completed, for they have not finished the redemption of their earth children, nor severed their connection with them. They are above "even the divine illusion of a Devachani," hence do not allow themselves to enter the joys of the state of Devachan (heaven world), for in it they would be cut off from their touch with humanity for ages. To keep from entering Devachan these Masters must therefore consciously guard their thoughts and not allow the Spiritual Mind (Higher Manas) to become fully united with the Spiritual Soul (Buddhi-Atma). Such Adepts consciously die to or withdraw from the Physical World leaving the physical body behind.

Such Masters are not "astral beings" in the ordinary sense of the term, nor are they merely disembodied Teachers, but are spiritually advanced Beings who have reached such a state of Mastery over earth conditions and forces as to pass through the gate of death at will and in full consciousness. They voluntarily withdraw from earth life that they may do a higher and more wide-spread work for humanity in these higher Realms, although they do not always confine their work to the astral, for "When an Adept reaches during his lifetime that state of holiness and purity that makes him 'equal to the angels' then at death his apparitional or astral body becomes as solid and tangible as was the late body, and is trans-

formed into the real man. The old physical body,
falling off like a cast-off serpent's skin, the body
of the 'new' man remains either visible or, at the
option of the Adept, disappears from view. . . . In
this case, after the physical translation of such a
saint or Bodhisatva, his astral principles cannot
be subjected to a natural dissolution like those of
any common mortal. They remain in our sphere
and within human attraction and reach. . . . Such
an Adept remains in the Astral (invisible) plane
connected with our earth, and henceforth moves
and lives in the possession of all his principles
except the Kama Rupa (body of desire) and the
Physical Body."[1]

There is another class of most spiritual and advanced Beings in this Realm, the Nirmanakayas or
Saviors. These are Masters who have reached the
highest stage of spiritual evolution possible either
on this or other planets without entering Nirvana
and losing all touch with the lower worlds of manifestations. These Great Ones voluntarily renounce
the bliss of Nirvana and retain "the influence of terrestrial attributes, however spiritualized, clinging to
that Self,"[2] for the purpose of retaining their touch
with humanity and becoming its Saviors. Under
these conditions "The Adept has the option of re-
nouncing conscious Nirvana and rest, to work on
earth for the good of mankind. This he can do in a
two-fold way; either, as above stated, by consolidat-

---

[1] *The Secret Doctrine*, Blavatsky, iii, 61-2, 372, 446.
[2] *Ibid.*, iii, 420.

ing his astral body into physical appearance, he can
reassume the self-same personality; or he can avail
himself of an entirely new physical body. . . . as
Shankarachraya is reported to have done."[3]

A true Nirmanakaya body, however, although
manifesting in the Astral World, is not an astral
or even a psychic body at all, but a *spiritual body*
which is born in the heart of the Adept while still in
the flesh, and which takes the form of the personality by first growing out through the marrow of the
bones and later extending out beyond them until it
permeates the entire body of flesh and ultimately
spiritualizes all its atoms. This process requires
many, many incarnations, but ultimately the body
thus spiritualized becomes no longer a mere physical body, nor even a purified astral body like that
of the Adept of the degree described above, but is
a redeemed and spiritual body in which its Master
can appear in any Realm or in any World at will.
For instance, by raising its vibrations above the
octave of the Physical World he would disappear
from physical sight and manifest in the astral, or by
again slowing down its vibrations—a process comparable to reducing the vibrations of water vapour
until they manifest as solid ice—could again appear
on earth in a body which to all appearances would
be a physical body, but which would not be so in so-
ber fact. This is the real meaning of the doctrine of

---

[3] *The Secret Doctrine*, Blavatsky, iii, 61-2.

the redemption (spiritualization) of the flesh. And
it is in such a spiritual body and by an analogous
process that an Avatar appears in the Physical
World.[4]

The ability of the Divine Teachers thus to appear
on earth in either of the two previously mentioned bodies or voluntarily to leave the Physical
World—at will the one through the gate of conscious death, the other through translation—is
so well known that allusions to it are found in all
scriptures and in many of the hero-myths of the
gods founding nations, giving mankind an alphabet, a numerical system, teaching him the use
of fire, etc., and then withdrawing to the heights
of some Olympus, Hemavat, Fujiyama or to the
heaven world as the case may be. Teachers who
have built up a Nirmanakaya body do not have to
wait for death to release them. For instance, we are
told that "Enoch walked with God; and he was not,
for God took him." The word Enoch is a generic
term used to designate all who have reached the
stage of Mastery in which they can withdraw from
the Physical World yet live and work in the higher
Realms of the astral. The Greek word "Enoichion,"
from which our word Enoch is derived, means "
the 'Inner Eye' or the Seer; in Hebrew, with the
help of the Masoretic points, it means the 'Initiator'
and 'Instructor'".[5] The story of Elijah who "went
up by a whirlwind into heaven" in a chariot

[4] See *The Voice of Isis*, Curtiss, Chapter X.
[5] *The Secret Doctrine*, Blavatsky, ii, 559.

of fire alludes to the same fact. St. Paul also alludes to it when he says: "He shall not see death." The same phenomena was again referred to when Jesus said: "He that believeth on me, though he were dead, yet shall he live; and whosoever liveth and believeth in me shall never die."[6]

---

[6] *St. John*, xi, 25-26.

CHAPTER XX

THE DIVINE OR ECSTATIC REALM

"Light is Cold Flame, and Flame is Fire, and Fire produces Heat, which yields Water—the Water of Life in the Great Mother. Father—Mother spin a Web, whose upper end is fastened to Spirit, the Light of the One Darkness, and the lower one to its shadowy end, Matter; and this Web is the Universe spun out of the two Substances made in One, which is Svabhavat."

Stanzas of Dzyan, iii, 9-10.

THIS Realm corresponds to the Divine or Formless World and to the seventh Principle (Atma) in man. As we have said elsewhere in describing the seven Principles of man,[1] Atma "is not a Principle of Man, but a Ray of pure Spirit from the Absolute." We therefore expect this Realm to be almost beyond the comprehension of the ordinary student, for its vibrations reach man through the heart and not through the brain. They are too high to be registered by the physical brain. In fact, as we have said of Atma, "It can contact the human body only as the higher astral centers are consciously awakened and

---

[1] *The Key to the Universe*, Curtiss, i, 266.

then made subservient to reaching into the higher
Realms where the Divine holds sway." Yet it
forever pours its forces upon man so that in it he
"lives and moves and has his being," although he
is not conscious of it.

This is the Realm which, because it corresponds
to the Divine or Formless World, is in very close
touch with it. Hence the undifferentiated Astral
Light, which in the Divine World is the first Light
of Creation, touching this Divine World when "God
said let there be light," enters into the Astral World
through this Divine Realm. Therefore in this Realm
of the Astral we find this Magical Agent *par excellence*, as we might say, at work. Since the Divine
World or Astral Light is often called the Sea of Fire,
primordial Ether, Akasia, Cosmic Electricity etc., in
the Divine Astral Realm this same astral light might
more fittingly be called "the fiery serpent;" for here
the pure undifferentiated Light, which is both positive and negative, is beginning to "Spin the Web"
which will ultimately be the Universe. Therefore
in its writhings and contortions it is allegorically
represented by the Hindus as the "Churning of the
Ocean by the Gods" and by other people as the
Great Serpent churning the ocean with its tail.

This idea of the Divine Light as a Serpent can
readily be understood when we realize that it is the
One Life or the Creative Magical Agent by which
the Cosmos came into being. This Fiery Serpent
is indeed the basis for the belief in both Heaven

and Hell, for it is the Light sent forth in the beginning out of which was created the cosmos; it is the One Life, hence is both creative, preservative and destructive. At its higher end it is joined to pure Spirit, the out-going Breath of Brahm, while at its lower end it manifests as the force which makes the trees grow and put forth blossoms, fruit to ripen and decay and all nature to respond to its force. In man it is his creative power, known in its lower aspect as sex-force, which is so little understood, and so sadly abused that from it man has indeed created all the hells in which his Soul has ever dwelt, yet out of a better understanding of it, when he becomes as the Gods knowing good as well as evil, he must create all the heavens to which his consciousness can respond. "Beginning with the pure Spiritual plane, it becomes grosser as it descends, until it becomes Maya or the tempting and deceitful Serpent on our plane."[2]

This Divine Realm may also be called the Mysterious Center in which this pure Divine Radiant Essence is broken up into duality to animate the grosser astral force; for in the Divine World it is but "the Shoreless Sea of Fire," while here it is the Fiery Serpent. A rather crude similie would be that this Realm is to the Cosmos what the stomach is to man, while the Fiery Serpent is like the intestine, *i.e.,* like the stomach it takes the Divine Sub-

---

[2] *The Secret Doctrine*, i, 103.

stance (astral light) given it by the gods and churns
and digests it, until it has been differentiated into its
constituents and is passed on into the Fiery Serpent
(intestine) to be assimilated by the lesser lives it is
to nourish.

"Thus this light, finally, is of the nature of fire,
the intelligent use of which warms and vivifies, and
the excess of which, on the contrary, dissolves and
annihilates. . . . This Light, therefore, inasmuch
as it is devouring, revengeful and fatal, would thus
really be hell-fire, the serpent of the legend; the
tormented errors of which it is full, the tears and the
gnashing of teeth of the abortive beings it devours,
the phantom of life that escapes them, and seems
to mock and insult their agony,[3] all this would be
the Devil or Satan indeed."[4]

This light might also be called the splendor of
the Divine Spiritual Sun going forth into manifestation, a ray of which is caught and imprisoned in the
highest substance of this most Spiritual Realm of
the Astral World where it begins its magical work of
creation; for the Astral Light is the Father-Mother of
all light. The sphere from which this radiant energy
or Astral Light comes is the Soul of the Universe
and the Life Principle of every living thing, from
the higher spiritual beings, down to man and the
lower kingdoms, just as we say the Higher Self is
the Soul of man. And just as the Higher Self sends

---

[3] As it manifests in the lower Realms, especially the Vital.
[4] *The Secret Doctrine*, Blavataky, ii, 538.

down a ray of itself into matter and clothes itself with a personality, so does the Astral Light send down a ray of itself and clothes it with the Substance of a Cosmos. It is "the matrix of the Universe, the Mysterium Magnum from which all that exists is born by separation. . . . it is the cause of existence; it fills all the infinite Space, is Space itself".[5]

When the Elohim said, "Let there be light," the great homegeneous but positive Father Ray was projected, and this Great Ray contained within itself the potencies of all the god-power that was to manifest in the Chaos and its resulting Cosmos. This ray, while relatively undifferentiated, was nevertheless dual. Hence as it came down into the realms of differentiation it necessarily manifested its two lower poles. The positive pole was active Divine Will and Wisdom (Life), its negative pole passive Divine Love and Compassion (Substance), which latter is the force of differentiation, since it is only through its feminine aspect that the ray could bring forth in the worlds of form.

It is in the Astral Light, as it is reflected from the Divine World into this Realm of the astral that the Soul of man receives its first differentiation *in form* as it descends into physical manifestation. "Because through, and in, the human form they (the Souls) will become progressive beings, whereas the nature

---

[5] *The Secret Doctrine*, Blavatsky, ii, 538.

of the Angel is purely intransitive; therefore Man
has in him the potency of transcending the faculties
of the Angels. . . . Finally, it is shown in every
ancient scripture and cosmogony that man evolved
primarily as a luminous incorporeal form, over
which, like molten brass poured into the model of
the sculptor, the physical frame of his body was
built by, through and from, the lower forms and
types of animal terrestrial life."[6]

Much that pertains to this Realm, because it is
a reflection of the Divine World, is hidden in deep
mystery, and like the Divine World itself with which
it is often confused, it is expressed in scriptural and
occult literature only in glyph, parable and symbol.
For instance, the Astral Light, as it manifests here,
is called the Dragon and the Seven-headed Serpent,
the heads being the seven Realms of the Astral
World. "And has been symbolized by every nation
as a Fiery Serpent breathing fire and light upon the
primeval water. . . . The Prince of the Air, of St.
Paul, is not the Devil, but the effect of the Astral
Light, as Eliphas Levi correctly explains."[7] The
Serpent is the universal symbol of the Astral Light
in its first differentiation, because its undulating
movements correspond to the vibratory motion of
the Astral Light in this Realm. This is one of the esoteric reasons back of all sacred dances, especially
the Egyptian and Chaldean, in which the hands and

---

[6] *The Secret Doctrine*, Blavatsky, ii, 118.
[7] *Ibid.*, ii, 509.

arms are made to undulate to simulate a serpent. In fact, the undulations of the arms and entire body had a mystic meaning and a magical effect, for these rhythmic motions when properly performed brought the devotees into rapport with vibrations of the Astral Light and thus tended to develop the psychic faculties and enabled them to see visions, etc. For it is by this light that all things in all Realms are brought into being. Such sacred dances have been practised in a more or less crude way in all religions and in all lands, notably among the Dervishes of Arabia, and the Indians of America, in both of whom they produced ecstasy, prophecy and sometimes trance and coma.

The Astral Light is the medium of magic *par excellence*. As described by Eliphas Levi: "This ambient and all-penetrating fluid, this ray detached from the (Central or Spiritual) Sun's splendour fixed by the weight of the atmosphere (?) and the power of external attraction. . . . the Astral Light, this electro-magnetic ether, this vital and luminous caloric, is represented on ancient monuments by the girdle of isis, which twines round two poles. . . . and in ancient theogonies by the serpent devouring its own tall, emblem of prudence and of Saturn (emblem of infinity, immortality, and Cronos—Time—not the God Saturn or the planet). It is the winged dragon of Medea, the double serpent of Caduceus, and the tempter of Genesis; but it is also the brazen snake of Moses

encircling the Tau. . . . lastly, it is the devil of
exoteric dogmatism, and is really the blind force
(it is not blind, and Levi knew it) which souls must
conquer, in order to detach themselves from the
chains of Earth; for if they should not, they will be
absorbed by the same power which first produced
them, and will return to the central and eternal fire."[8]

This utterance, while very cryptic, is nevertheless quite simple if we bear in mind that the Astral
Light is Divine Creative Substance. Hence, to
conquer it the Souls which were formed from this
Divine Creative Substance must learn to manifest
it in the flesh and permeate the physical matter of
their bodies with it. In other words, they must learn
to let their Light shine before men, and also be perfect even as their Father-in-heaven (in this sense the
Astral Light from which the Soul is differentiated)
is perfect. If we refuse to do this and so intensify the
density of the physical body that the Light cannot
illuminate it, then that Light (which is the life of the
Soul) will be withdrawn and once more enter the
Divine Worlds as undifferentiated Spiritual Light
or be indrawn into the bosom of the Father of Light
or will be broken up and return to the "central fire"
from whence it came. This fire is central in that, being the highest Realm of the Astral World, it stands
between the Physical and the Divine Worlds.

---

[8] *The Secret Doctrine*, Blavatsky, i, 275.

"If the student bears in mind that there is but one Universal Element, which is infinite, unborn and undying, and that all the rest—as in the world of phenomena—are but so many various differentiated aspects and transformations (correlations, they are now called) of that One, from macrocosmical down to microcosmical effects, from super-human down to human and sub-human beings, the totality in short of objective existence—then the first and chief difficulty will disappear and Occult Cosmology may be mastered."[9]

The Astral Light, being the radian of the Spiritual Sun which, like the Physical Sun, while in the heavens yet pervades all forms of life and fills all space, is the one medium of Spirit and Life in all. Hence the art of Divine or White Magic consists in the ability to find this Light, first within yourself, then in all mankind, in all nature and in all substances, and correlate your consciousness with it. Since it is the inner essence of all things it is possible to perceive the essence of all things in this Light, which is therefore sometimes called the Light of Nature. But this can be done only through the use of the Soul powers. No being, astral or otherwise, can do this for you. Your Teacher may point out the way and lay down the rules, but your own consciousness must dwell in the Light and be one with this great and magic Agent. Then all Divine Magic is

---

[9] *The Secret Doctrine*, Blavatsky, i, 104.

possible. "Such processes take place according to law. You will learn the law by which these things are accomplished, if you learn to know yourself. You will know it by the power of the spirit that is in yourself, and accomplish it by mixing your spirit with the essence which comes out of yourself. If you wish to succeed in such a work you must know how to separate spirit and life in nature, and, moreover, to separate the Astral Soul in yourself and make it tangible, and then the substance of the Soul will appear visibly and tangibly, rendered objective by the power of the spirit."[10]

---

[10] *The Secret Doctrine*, Blavatsky, footnote to 538.

CHAPTER XXI

INDEPENDENT COMMUNICATIONS

An Aviator's Great Adventure
The Annunciation

AUTHOR'S NOTE. Since the publication of the First Edition many readers have asked for further examples of Independent Communications. The following specimens will serve to show the possibilities and range of such communications, varying as they do from the Young Aviator, who could not be convinced that he had left the physical body, to the high intelligence of the great Angel of the planet Saturn.

These communications are all given practically in the wording received and without the intellectual revision, elaboration and polishing which most literary efforts receive before publication. All were received by Mrs. Curtiss while in full consciousness and often while busy with household or other affairs, as for example, the message from the Young Aviator which was received while riding in an automobile. This shows that it is the state of consciousness that is essential, not the time or place, although these may often be helpful in placing the mind of the recipient in a tranquil state in which it can the more easily respond to the higher states of consciousness and to the Intelligences of the higher worlds.

AN AVIATOR'S GREAT ADVENTURE

The following incident well illustrates the great difficulty many who pass out of the body suddenly have in realizing their real condition. It also illustrates the Independent Method of communion with those who are not in the physical body. The message was from a young aviator of great prominence whose aeroplane was shot down during a fight with a number of German machines. The message was received on July 18th, 1918, before his death had been officially corroborated. While traveling twenty-five miles an hour in an automobile between Philadelphia and New York a young man whom she had never seen before suddenly presented himself to the inner vision of Mrs. Curtiss, dressed in full aviation costume. Although Mrs. Curtiss had never seen his picture she was able to identify it positively when it was shown her later. The dialogue which follows was written down from memory soon after and as accurately as possible, so that the essence of the conversation can be vouched for even though the exact wording cannot. The initials Y.A. will represent the young aviator and Dr. C. will stand for Dr. Curtiss who carried on the conversation, Mrs. Curtiss repeating the questions and answers from one to the other in full consciousness while the automobile was speeding along without stop.

As soon as the name of the young man was given to Mrs. Curtiss, Dr. Curtiss challenged him as follows:

Dr. C. "Are you. . . in very truth?"

The young man stood before Mrs. C. with a bright cheery smile and in answer to the challenge as to his identity took his aviator's bonnet in his right hand and made a sweeping bow that was particularly graceful, yet boyish and unstudied.

Y.A. "Yes I am. . . at your service."

Dr. C. "We are glad to meet you. Is there anything we can do for you?"

Y.A. "Thank you, no. I am meeting with so many strange adventures I like to talk them over."

Dr. C. "How did you come to meet with us?"

Y.A. "Oh, I just met up with you and felt attracted."

Dr. C. "Then you have really passed over?"

Y.A. in surprise. "Passed over what?"

Dr. C. "Passed out of your physical body. You are now in what many people would call heaven."

Y.A. quickly. "Heaven nothing! And I know I'm not in the other place!"

Dr. C. "Of course you are not dead, but you have left your physical body."

Y.A. "Oh, no. I have just had a wonderful adventure, that's all. I've discovered a country that's not on the map and I mean to spend some time here and study it. Then when I've got the facts I'll come back and tell the boys."

Dr. C. letting the point pass. "Tell us how you got there."

Y.A. "Well, I was flying and we got into a bit of a row with the Boches and I felt a sting in my head and my machine began to fall."

Dr. C. "What did you do then?"

Y.A. "Why, I jumped out. I always felt I could fly myself. Only instead of falling down I flew up here."

Dr. C. "How do you explain that?"

Y.A. "Well, there are lots of strange things happen to an aviator. I had always felt I could fly. Ever since I was a small boy I had dreams of flying through the air and since I joined the flying corps the feeling came back so strong that I had hard work to keep from stepping out of the machine and trying it. So when I saw I had lost control of the machine I jumped out as I had planned, and, just as I expected, I could fly and went straight up until I landed here safe and sound."

Dr. C. "Of course it is only your body that is dead, not you."

Y.A. "But my body is not dead. If I had struck the earth of course I would have been smashed, but I never struck the earth. I came up here."

Dr. C. "While you are not dead, for there is no death, nevertheless you have put off your body of flesh and are now living in a finer, more ethereal body just like the physical."

Y.A. "Atta-boy! Stop trying to kid me! I never

was a good one to kid. I've got my body just as substantial as ever. I've got on my aviator's uniform and I fill it out all round. You couldn't put a uniform on a ghost, could you?"

Dr. C. "Well, if you will read our book on the subject along with your father you will find it all explained."

Y.A. "Well, when you make your point I'll admit it. But you've got to prove it."

Dr. C. "Were you at all afraid when you began to fall?"

Y.A. "Afraid nothing! I never knew what fear was. I've proved there was nothing to fear."

Dr. C. "What do you eat up there?"

Y.A. "Come to think of it I haven't eaten since I've been here. But then I often go without eating for quite a while and don't mind it. Now you mention it I do feel hungry. Guess I'll go and get some chow right now."

Y.A. after a lapse of a few minutes reopens the conversation. "Well, here I am again, and I've proved it."

Dr. C. "Proved what?"

Y.A. "Why, that I'm not dead. I've not only had a swell meal, but I've met up with an old chum who is in the service and we both had a fine chow. Now where is a ghost going to put a big meal like that? Does a ghost have a stomach? Ha! Ha! And my chum is just as alive as I am. I pinched him to see and he hollered 'Ouch'! What do you say to that?"

Dr. C. "Did you pay for your meal?"

Y.A. "Sure I did."

Dr. C. "Where did you get the money?"

Y.A. "I don't know. I didn't have my purse in my uniform and yet somehow I paid for the meal. Look here, Doctor, I'm willing to play this game fair. If you can prove to me that I'm a ghost I'll admit it, but if I can prove that I'm alive you must admit it too."

Dr. C. "I did not say you were dead or that you had no body, only that you had lost your physical body."

Y.A. "Well, there are a lot of strange things happen to an aviator. Any of the boys will tell you that. I believe that I have simply had a wonderful adventure, and those who have had any experience in the air will agree that there are more wonderful things happen than you could ever dream of on the earth. I've simply found a new way to escape being wrecked and as soon as I study it out I'm coming back and tell the boys how to do it, so they can fly without their machines too, and so save millions in equipment."

Dr. C. "Have you been home to see your father yet?"

Y.A. "No. I'm going to take a little furlough and explore the country up here before I go home. I don't want to go home to my father with any fairy tales. He will want facts and I'd rather wait until I can talk sense and prove it than simply repeat what you tell me."

Dr. C. "Where do we seem to be now?"

Y.A. surprised. "Why, you are up here with me. You belong in this country."

Dr. C. "No. You are mistaken. We are simply with you in consciousness. Physically we are in our auto traveling toward New York at twenty-five miles an hour."

Y.A. "Well, I'll have to be going if you don't stop trying to kid me."

Dr. C. "Did you feel much pain when you were hit?"

Y.A. "No. Just a sort of a sting. I've often had more pain in my head when the cold wind was blowing in my ears?'

Dr. C. "Well, any time we can be of help to you we would be glad to have you come again."

Y.A. "Thanks. I'm going to look into the matter. But I'm not going home just yet. My father would want me to be doing my duty and finding out this new invention of how we can fly without our machines so I can give it to the government. My mother wouldn't want me to come home just to be petted. This is my chance. And I'm not going back until I've found things out. Because I might not be able to find my way back here again. So long."

Note. Some days later. We are told that the Y.A. will soon return (incarnate), possibly within twenty or thirty years, to complete his life-cycle, as his one great desire is to perfect the aeroplane for the benefit of his country. Because of his unselfish eagerness to be of use to his country and to mankind, without a thought of benefit to himself, he will soon be led into the Pattern Museum[1] where he will study the perfected aeroplanes of the ancient Atlanteans, so that when he returns he may help to perfect the dynaspheric motor which will draw continuous and unlimited power directly from the etheric forces of the air.

The Annunciation

Reach out your hands, blessings are falling.
    Open your can, the angels are calling.
Open your hearts, O children of earth!
    Wake! For today comes the heavenly birth.

Over this land there is centered a star.
    That reaches to earth its rays from afar.
Lift up your brows and a diadem weave
    Out of the star-dust, sorrow's reprieve.

Onward courageously walk through your task,
    Only the guerdon of Love shall you ask.
For unto you this day is it given
    To sit at meat with your Father-in-Heaven.

---

[1] See page 105.

CHAPTER XXII

INDEPENDENT COMMUNICATIONS
(Continued)

A Message from Lincoln
A Prophecy of the Aquariun Age
A Vision of the Coming

A Message From Lincoln

A Call to America

(Note. The following message, first published in *Azoth Magazine* of May, 1917, and reprinted here with their permission, we feel to have been not only a prophecy of what America was soon to face and accomplish, but was an indication that the great soul of Abraham Lincoln was bringing to bear upon the leaders of our beloved country the same influence which this message expresses, and through that influence had much to do in guiding the nation and awakening in our broad land the old time enthusiasm and determination to fight, not only for Liberty, but to sustain in the world at large all the high ideals for which Americanism stands. Of course this was before America entered the war and while pacifism and Pro-Germanism were rampant. *The Authors*)

OUT of the great mass of omens which occurred just prior to the present Great War the following striking ones may be called to mind. "At the celebration of Sedan Day (September 1) at the Saxon town of

Artern, in 1911, hundreds of the inhabitants had
gathered in the large square which has Bismarck's
statue in the center, when suddenly the sword which
the figure of the maker of modern Germany holds
extended at length, dropped from the statue's hand
and fell noisily to the ground. The fall of the sword
was immediately followed by that of the sword arm
of the Imperial Chancellor. In the next year, 1912,
the Balkan War broke out, which was the precursor
of the present crisis. About the same time, or shortly
after, as one of the results of an earthquake, which
took place that autumn on the Continent of Europe,
a colossal statue of Germania was overthrown at
Constance. Another even more significant result of
this earthquake, in the eyes of the superstitious, was
the rending of the solid masonry towers of the Burg
Hohenzollern, the ancestral castle of the reigning
house. A further omen of disaster, to Belgium, was
the cracking of the famous Rouland bell in the
belfry of Ghent, which has been held to symbolize
for many centuries past the spirit of Flemish liberty.
On July 22 of the year 1914 it cracked and broke
when ringing. This incident was regarded at the
time as a dire omen of evil."[1]

In view of the above incidents, the damage which
our own Statue of Liberty sustained from the missiles
which rained upon it after the explosion of several
barges of ammunition which blew up in New York
harbor on the night of July 30, 1916, may fairly be

---

[1] See *Prophecies and Omens of the Great War*, Shirley, 50, 51.

considered a serious omen for America, in view of the laws underlying such phenomena revealed in the following message, and especially in view of the fact that the missiles were fashioned by her own sons.

There were three of us seated before the glowing logs of the fireplace on the evening of Tuesday, February 27, 1917, and we had been quietly discussing present world conditions when suddenly the glowing fire seemed to fade away or be obscured by a thick chilling fog. Wondering at this strange phenomenon, and shivering as we continued to peer into its thick gray depths, two of those present, *while in full waking consciousness*, began to see the faint outlines of the Statue of Liberty appear through the fog, but corroded, bedraggled and forlorn. Instead of the heart thrill that had invariably marked our sight of that great symbol of our country's ideals, this vision brought with it the most depressing sense of impending disaster. And as we continued to gaze spellbound at the singular scene, the familiar figure of Abraham Lincoln seemed to emerge from the fog above the statue. His head was bowed in sorrow. His face was wan and haggard as from carrying a great burden of care and anxiety, and in his eyes was the deep heart-sorrow and suffering of a consuming sadness as of one whose highest ideals had been scorned and trampled under foot by those he loved best.

Observing our attention, he raised his head, and with right arm uplifted, his lips began to move and we seemed to hear his voice, in tones of tragic sadness whose pathos seemed to melt our hearts, giving us the following message which he begged us to transmit to his beloved people.

"America can retain the freedom of the seas and her place among the nations only through a recognition of the necessity of building a Statue of Liberty, not only in the harbor of her greatest city, but by lifting up a Statue of Liberty in its true sense in the hearts of her people. Only thus can she ever take her true place.

"The proud boast of America that she is 'the Land of Liberty and the Home of the Free' is symbolized in her great Statue of Liberty in New York harbor. It is most significant that in this age and day America is losing her high ideals as the land of liberty and the home of the brave. No longer does she hold up the torch of Liberty to enlighten the world, but crouches behind her own bulwarks crying 'Peace! Peace!' when there is no peace, drawing her garment before her face as her sisters and brothers pass by in their misery and agony, saying: 'It is nothing to me. We are the land of the free.'

"Almost at the beginning of the crisis in the affairs of our beloved country, for which we weep, a most untoward accident seemed to befall our Statue of Liberty. You will doubtless recall the fire which caused the explosion of the barges laden with ammunition along the New Jersey shore. To one who pays attention to the events of life; who realizes that every great national event, such as the erection of a great statue which symbolizes the ideals of the nation, marks an epoch in its history, such an accident has a profound significance. For all the forces of the air, of the elements and of nature combine to respect that symbol and force those who have erected it to live up to its ideals. And when these ideals are belittled the elements combine to show to man that something is vitally wrong. Therefore this bombardment and damage to the Statue of Liberty should have been a significant omen of that which occurred in the higher realms.

"O America! Thou beloved of my soul! Thou for whom the blood of the brave and the true has been shed! Thou for whose ideals great souls have struggled and perished and attained! Where is thy Liberty? Where is thy Freedom? Like the mist upon the harbor such a little thing serves to blot out from your eyes the wonderful Statue of Liberty! O decadent nation, wrapped in thy slumber of sophistry! lulled into a distracted sleep by man's greed, dissension and the machinations of thine enemies! How long think you this condition can endure?

"Brave sons are awakening in this great day and are already turning their eyes to your Flag of Freedom, crying out for a leader. Where is the Man of Destiny who shall recognize his right to be the deciding factor in this world's confused day of reckoning? Where is the brave and great Leader who shall call out the Sons of America to uphold the institutions of Divine Liberty and Protection and Freedom?

"O cringing nation! I know you not. O effeminate and degenerate rulers! I recognize you not!

"Souls of America, ARISE! AWAKE! Throw off this slothful death-gripping insomnia of unrest!

"Look into the eyes of the true Statue of Liberty! that which exists in the higher realms; that which is the Mother who gave thee birth and suckled thee at her breasts. Look deep into her eyes. See her gazing far out and away from your own land into the distant corners of the world. Then look around her feet. See the many of her seeming own, the poor, the hungry, the suffering, and the lost of all lands, clinging for protection beneath her skirts!

"How your hearts thrilled when she sheltered in her arms the negro slave and said 'He *shall* be free!' Yet look yonder. See the slaves! Hear the cries! Listen to the agony of your brothers and sisters across the sea! Where is the strong arm that can protect? Where is the mother-love that can shelter?

"O America! America! No longer, no longer the Land of the Free, but the land of greed and selfishness, of sophistry, of dissension among yourselves. Who shall save you? To whom shall we look for succor? Shall we tear down our Statue of Liberty? Shall we allow the elements to destroy it? Yes. Yes. It cannot stand unless the land it guards be true to its ideals.

"Children of unrest! Children of unrest! Would to God that the cannon's roar might wake you from your slothful sleep and self-seeking. Would to God some great call should come to you. Yet I would not that the call should be 'Save yourselves.' Oh no! Save your brothers, your sisters, the world! Stop this carnage like the strong giant that you are. Take your stand for principle and for right. And strike with the strength of the great Powers that are back of you; the Powers that won freedom for you from the tyranny of the old world. Everywhere you are answered: 'Know your strength! Win freedom for the world.'

"Can you not see the great forces gathered on the higher planes which are seeking to send into your hearts, Oh children of men, the old-time cry of FREEDOM?

"O God, send us the Man of Destiny! Send us the Man of Destiny!

"Has the scroll been obliterated? the great scroll on which it has been written by the hand of Divine Law that this nation is destined to become the leader of the world! No hand but the hand of its own sons could obliterate it.

"Leaders are not made by money, by greed, avarice, dissension, deception and underhanded dealings.

"The Spirit of America lies crushed and bleeding. The cannons that have roared on the fields of battle have gone through her heart. The torpedoes that have sunk brave ships without warning have entered into her bosom and have sunk her beneath the waves of life. But is there no life left in this corpse? Cry out to the Lord of Battles for strength, for understanding and for truth. Let go the childish cry for

Peace, Peace, when there is no peace. Can you be saved and hear the whole world groan? Can you be great and all the rest annihilated? Is this greatness the greatness of saving your own skin? or is it the greatness to Dare, to Do and to Die? And greater still, to come forth in the strength and power of the Lord of Hosts, knowing your destiny; recognizing that for which you were born in blood in a fight for Liberty, and declare yourself for Liberty and the Enlightening of the World!

"O America! America! Thou art the Man! Thou art the Nation of Destiny! Dare you deny it? Dare you hide when cannons roar? Dare you cringe when blood flows? Dare you doubt your high destiny?

"O America! America! Nation of my love! Art thou fallen! Art thou fallen?"

A PROPHECY OF THE AQUARIAN AGE

The Moon, a pure, cold, chaste goddess, was wooed and won by the Sun God. He was warm and ardent and his embraces were irresistible. From their union was born the wonderful goddess Urania. She is more beautiful and more chaste than her mother, yet more warm and ardent than her father. Her force is so great that the Children of Earth are not able to greet her, for they cannot endure the light of her countenance.[2]

---

[2] Uranus affects the horoscopes of mortals largely through her effect on other planets, for she is a Ruler among ruling planets.

All through the ages she has walked in darkness. A thick veil covers her face and thick clouds compass her about. She is enshrouded in mystery. Even the Sun God her father can scarce find her.

From time to time as she walks her appointed path she crosses the paths of the other gods (planets).[3] And as she walks the heavens her footprints become centers of force. And along and within their radiations blossoms of wondrous potency spring into being.

Although she is invisible the gods feel her approach and are thrilled with expectant love. The chords of their hearts are moved with a mighty force, prophetic and inspiring. Even the far-off Children of Earth catch the vibrations of that thrill and in every heart attuned to love's higher chords there awakens an answering wave of joy from whence unknown. And in every Soul who has sacrificed on love's altar, who has suffered and lost, there is born with that cosmic thrill a new conception of Love Divine.

Clothed in impenetrable mystery, bold indeed is the mortal who dares to lift even a corner of her veil.

Yet the time[4] draws quickly nigh when her cloak will drop from her shoulders and she will no longer be shrouded in mystery. The veil will be lifted from her

---

[3] These terms refer to the ruling Planetary Deities, the great spiritual entities who have charge of the various planets, "The seven angels that stand before the throne."

[4] The Aquarian Age which we have now just entered, during which Uranus is the esoteric ruler.

face and mankind will marvel at her wondrous beauty. Even now on earth there is found one here and there who boldly climbs to the seat of the Sun God and lights his Torch of Truth in those golden rays. As torch after torch flames out into the darkness the dank mists of ignorance will melt and chill darkness will die in the embrace of Light. Then will mankind seek out the goddess Urania in her hidden ways and daring to lift her veil will bask unharmed in the unspeakable loveliness of her smile. Then all who have given up the great gift of love for duty or conscience's sake will find it again, purified and sanctified by her potent force; grown sweet and fragrant under her cloak. Then will their own come to them, whom none can take away.

The time will come when the world shall see this goddess sitting upon the golden throne of her father the Sun God, with the silver scepter of her mother in her right hand. Behind her will stand her faithful henchman Neptune, with his Rod of three-fold Power in his hand, ready to defend her or to punish any mortal over-bold. On her right hand will stand the god Jupiter, and on her left hand Saturn, while prone at her feet will lie the beautiful Venus who has yielded up her life only to find it in more abundance in the smile of her elder sister Urania. And as Venus' valiant lover Mars stoops to lift her, he places his arms around her and draws her close to his heart. With the tears of passion dried from out their eyes so shall they stand, like two innocent love-children, all smiles

and beguilings, in the pure radiant Light of the
goddess Urania.

A VISION OF THE COMING

The following is the description of a vision of
the coming Avatar recently seen by Mrs. Curtiss.[5] It
is written down verbatim as it was realized by her
consciousness with no attempt to put it into literary form. This original form is reproduced just as
it was received for every expression has a special
creative potency:

The word is spoken.

The sable curtains of the darkness part.
He who dwells in everlasting radiance comes
    forth.
With Him, rank on rank, angelic Beings move in
    ever-widening circles.
Transcendent, ever-changing hues of Light with
    blinding radiance intoxicate the air.
From angelic harps rich melody rolls onward.
The very echoes of yon planet, earth, tremble with
    ecstasy
And with delirious joy sink into silence profound
    and awesome.

What bodes it me, an humble child of earth, that I
    behind the veil may glimpse?
Who art Thou, Lord? whom to Thy shepherds thus
    appeareth?

---

[5] First issued to *The Order of Christian Mystics* in June, 1917.

I dare not look.
My weary world-worn eyes I cannot lift.
Yet rests thy crown of glory on my brow.

"Light of the World, forever shining,
    Though streaming tears thy radiance hide.
Sun of my Soul, forever near
    Lift up my heart in adoration
And there abide for aye.

Deep in my empty heart ent'ring;
    All Love Divine and Wisdom cent'ring,
My Savior, Lord, I'm lost in Thee.

Empty Thine arms, with blessings laden,
    Grant me the boon to bear them on."

Thus spake my Soul.

From out the Silence, rolling thunder.
And many Voices cried Amen! Amen!

The heavenly hosts are stilled as Thou draw'st near.
Aye! E'en the harmony divine in silence dies when
    Thou appear'st.
Grant me to rest in Thy bright shining.

Forth from the hosts angelic a Being speaks:

"Still, O earth, thy heart! The Lord Christ cometh.
He passeth by; and thrills the farthest region
Where waves of death beat earth's dark shore.
The darkness flees, by glory vanquished.
The day of blood and steel and death is o'er."

Silent, still and empty. Naught of earth remaining.
Only Thy joy and peace and love abiding.
Sun of my Soul, shine on! Shine on!

CHAPTER XXIII

INDEPENDENT COMMUNICATIONS
(Continued)

A Message from Saturn
The Garden of Prayers

A MESSAGE FROM SATURN

I AM the first and the last. I am the beginning and the end. I am the dread Guardian of the Threshold. I come to you with gaunt and pallid face, cold and lifeless as the dead. I stretch out my arms as a barrier to stop your onward journey. Come, look into my dead and lusterless eyes. Look upon my ghastly countenance if ye dare! Look me in the face and recognize me for what I am; for until ye can meet me face to face and know and conquer me ye cannot pass.

I am the Great Initiator. I stand upon the Threshold. I am the Great Tester, the glass which mirrors back each mortal's own creations, his Dweller which each Neophyte must face and recognize before I let him pass.

I am Saturn the great Reaper. I am he who binds, who congeals, who solidifies. I am he that seemeth like a corpse; for I am all that is dead and lifeless. Look! Look in my dead face and recognize me! What do I mean? I am the sadness and the darkness and the coldness of death, the fear of which each Neophyte must face and overcome.

The planetary forces that gave ye life push ye ever onward and outward on the great Spiral of Life.[1] Day after day ye are urged farther and farther away, onward and outward, until ye reach my domain. Here I stretch out my grizzled arms and bid ye halt; for I am he that saith: "Thus far shalt thou go and no farther." Not even the forces of the gods can pass my domain unchallenged.

Each planetary force hath carried ye a space and given ye of its guerdon of power and wisdom and truth until the confines of the Spiral of Life are reached. And I, what have I to give? I give ye naught. I bid ye face thyself. Here do I meet ye and say, "Thus far shalt thou go." Stand and look me in the face! Can ye stand still while thy vitals are frozen by my icy breath? For I am the wintertime when all is cold and dead. And I must be met and passed before the spring can come. Out of this ordeal must ye gather the power that binds together into an entity all the forces ye have received from the planetary gods.

Are ye proof against my frozen breath? Can ye bear to have thine ideals shattered, thine advance retarded, all that seemed good and true filched from thy

---

[1] See lesson *Spiral of Life*, Curtiss.

grasp? Can ye meet these tests undaunted, seize them and turn defeat into victory, discouragement into power? Can ye be still and reach my stage of calm contemplation while all that ye loved and believed in seems to wither and die in thy sight? Not until ye have seized from me my weapons and gained my power can ye pass this point (Initiation) and go onward.

Think ye there is no reason why I, Saturn, stand at the Threshold? at the outpost of life and evolution? In the foundation of the universe it was I who made the cosmic center and gave the stability and inertia upon which the other planetary forces might act. Mine was the force sent out in the beginning and mine shall be the last to return; the power of holding still, of being fixed and immovable. I am the dot that expanded into the circle[2] which contained and circumscribed all that could come forth in a cosmic manifestation; the aura of a man; that which limits and confines his life-forces and prevents them from being dissipated; the measure of a man.

In the solar system the planets are ever sending their forces outward into space, and were it not for me they would go onward beyond the confines of this system and be dissipated. But when they reach my domain I stop them and say: "So far shalt thou go." I build a wall about the universe and turn back the separate forces and blend them into one. This wall creates form and number.

---

[2] See *The Key to the Universe*, Curtiss, Chapter 5.

I am he that bindeth and that is bound with the three bands.[3] I hold the three forces that bind body, soul and spirit. The force of this calm that can bind and hold ye must learn; for as long as anything can upset and disturb thy calm ye cannot pass on. For I, Saturn, am the Guardian of the Portals.

The planetary gods lead ye down the Spiral of Life until the last round is reached and there stand I. If it were not for my outstretched arms ye might be pushed over the edge of the Spiral into the Great Abyss and be lost in the Outer Darkness.[4] Yet ye must face this Abyss and calmly contemplate its depths and lose not thy balance ere ye have strength to turn and walk upward inside the Spiral. Then thy path is no longer outward but ever inward where ye shall feed on the inner Essence of Life.

The Soul who has dared to meet and face me and wrest from me my power and walk upward within the Spiral, for him do I gather up all the planetary forces and send them back to him as helpers, as the dot expands into the circle. "As above, so below." As in the cosmos, so in man. For him shall I no longer be Saturn the Reaper, but will be crowned as Cronus, God of Time; for he who has reached this step is ruler over time. But ye must see the outward face of Death the Reaper ere ye can recognize my true face.

Then do I become benign and my power is the power

---

[3] The three Rings of Saturn.
[4] The dead region where the forces of one planet end and ere those of another begin.

of wisdom. But ye must be able to correlate with my force before ye can climb the Inner Path. Ye cannot pass on until ye have culled from me the lesson of stability and the wisdom Cronus alone can teach. Then shall ye conquer through discernment.

I am the melancholia of the world which if not conquered leads on to insanity and death. Ye must face the world with death, pallid and stark, standing at thine elbow. Ye must become as dead to the changing tides of the world and of man's changing affairs as though in the grave.

O sons of earth, like Saturn ye are bound with three rings, hand and foot; body, Soul and Spirit. These rings are the three days in the tomb.[5] These ye must break through, and conquer the force that binds ye, a day for a ring. These binding conditions must hold ye until the very force which bound ye is turned into the stability of the indomitable will of undaunted courage and unquenchable faith; the faith that has touched the confines of life and has penetrated its Mysteries. And when I am conquered ye will find me Lucifer the brilliant Angel of Light, the bright Star of the Morning who shall make all things plain unto thee.

But to know me ye must meet me face to face. Ye must see my gaunt arms reaching out for ye and boldly walk into those ghastly limbs and tear the mask from my dead and frozen face; must warm my cold heart with the warmth of thy breasts. Come to

---

[5] See lesson *Three Days in the Tomb*, Curtiss.

me and wrench from me the power of Silence; of
quiet contemplation; of standing still. To know me
ye must study me and find out my secret.

I come not to give ye my force. I cannot. Ye must
wrest it from me in battle. I am the dread God of
the Threshold guarding all Wisdom! How dare ye
pass me? I am placed here at the end of things to
weigh and measure ye all. After ye pass me there
is no other. Ye are free to pass onward and inward
toward the Fount of all Light and Wisdom. No more
can the forces assail ye nor the terrors of the Abyss
draw ye down; for ye have passed the edge and are
inside the Spiral and turn back only of thine own
free will.

But ye dare not pass me until ye meet me; until
ye feel the grip of my grizzly hands at thy throat
shutting off thy life's breath; until ye feel my icy
breath on thy cheek. Thus must ye wrestle. If I
conquer, down into the Abyss ye go, to begin over
again thy Cycle of Manifestation. But if ye conquer
I am thy Servant and Savior.

I am he who was sent out in the beginning, hence
I am called Lucifer, Star of the Morning. I am he
of whom it was said, "I beheld Satan as lightning
fall from heaven."[6] I am the angel of *Revelation*
who goeth forth to weigh and take the measure of
all men. For no man is a MAN until he has been
measured; until he has cognized my force and has
gained its stability.

---

[6] *St. Luke* x, 18.

THE GARDEN OP PRAYERS

Invocation. *Evening Prayer.* O divine and loving Father, as we rest through the darkness on thy breast, help us to draw close to thee in love, and to realize the almighty power of thy divine Son filling and comforting us. For as the earth and air retain the magnetic and life-giving forces of the sun to bring forth for the new day as it withdraws each night, so may we retain in our Souls through the darkness the light and warmth of his shining, knowing that as the sun rises for the new day we too shall rise stronger, truer, sweeter and more beautiful because we have rested in thy love in abiding faith and trust.

In the fair Fields of Asphodel prayers grow like flowers. Some are prayers of anguish from hearts that are breaking. And, oh, they are crimson red! Yet out of the center of each a golden stamen points upward, bringing down the Divine Radiance into the very heart of passion or sorrow, stilling them.

There are the prayers that are lisped by baby lips, "God bless mama and papa" These are tiny violets and daisies, so sweet and pure and beautiful, nodding their little heads in hundreds of thousands all over the grass.

Then there are stately lilies, so pure and white. They are the prayers of the saints whose hearts have been purified from all earth desires. There are beautiful roses too. These are the prayers of those passionate lovers who have learned to know and to dwell in beautiful love. They pour out their hearts in adoration like the perfume of the rose. Oh! How beautiful are these fields!

Prayers for success are grand and stately flowers with long stalks standing up straight and high, with flowers all down the sides, many, many flowers. Some are white with golden centers. And some are purple and blue and crimson according to their ideal. But the most beautiful are those that have within their hearts little golden stamens. And every time the Winds of Heaven blow the bright dust of their golden pollen showers down upon mankind. Why, you ask? Because these are the prayers that have asked success and blessing for all the world. So the showers of golden dust fall upon all. And where'er they fall and find lodgment they bring happiness and success.

Selfish prayers for mere worldly success are not allowed to grow in these fields. We call them weeds. We go out and pull them up and cast them back to earth and say to the children of earth: "Take back your prayers, they are not worthy of place in this Garden. They come back to you to be readjusted. Gather them up. They belong only in the soil of earth. Readjust them." For only when so readjusted can such prayers grow into beautiful flowers in the Fields of Asphodel.

Sometimes selfish prayers force success, like hot-house flowers of untimely bloom. These the angels pluck and throw back to earth. Such success as may thus be gained is but of the earth and only for the moment: only while the flowers thus plucked endure. They have no root in heaven.

The prayers that demand and demand and insist upon their fulfillment without saying, "Not my will, but thine be done," are also weeds, bitter weeds and rank. Their answer seems to come because they grow a little, but their flowers soon fall and give place to bitter fruit which often purges those who planted and must eat.

The prayers that the Great Gardener loves are those which create the beautiful Flowers of Immortality. They are prayers of gratitude and thankfulness; the recognition of what you really are; the accepting of all your blessings with joy. Those are the greatest prayers of all, the prayers of thankfulness and joy; when you accept your blessings and realize how your Father loves you and how glad he is to see that you understand and permit him to help you.

Take then your blessings and laugh back into His face like glad flowers nodding joyously back to the sun. Say, "O my Father! I am so happy because you love me and give me that which you know is best for me, except when I demand for self alone."

CHAPTER XXIV

INDEPENDENT COMMUNICATIONS
(Continued)

The Message of the Sphinx
The Curtain

THE MESSAGE OF THE SPHINX

ONE evening while sitting around a blazing
wood fire there was placed in the hands of Mrs.
Curtiss a small stone image of the sphinx which
had been brought to her direct from a royal tomb
in Egypt. Holding it lightly and unthinkingly in her
hands and while conversing about Egypt, suddenly
the following psychometric message poured into
her consciousness and was written down verbatim
as it fell from her lips.[1]

Out of the distant past when the forces of the
world were gathered into a mighty storm there was
a message, a mighty message, given to humanity
and embodied in imperishable symbols.

All the kingdoms of the earth gave to this Great
Mystery something of their forces and experience.
Out of the Earth rose great animals, strong and

---

[1] Also see lesson *The Message of the Sphinx*, Curtiss.

mighty to labor. They lived and died and while forgotten they left behind a force which was Strength and Power and Endurance. This formed the hind part of the Great Mystery.

Upon this, like a mighty thing it crouches, lying down in patience, resting in powerful strength; subject to the mighty dictates of the Law of Time; waiting for the hour to strike when the power and strength and patience shall be utilized.

That mighty Image of Eternal Creation shall arise. On its shoulders powerful wings are spread; for out of the Air, like great birds soaring in the heavens, comes the force which we know as the awful longing to penetrate beyond the clouds; to explore the heights; to bring back an answer from the invisible Portals of Eternity. It is this unanswerable longing that is forever expressed in the outstretched wings.

On its forepart are breasts as of a woman, symbol of the force which goes ever on and on, ever feeding, ever bringing forth; patiently giving and waiting; waiting for the end when these creatures she has suckled shall become the Lords of Creation. And the cry goes forth:

O the force of Mother-love! O Eternal Nourisher who hath poured forth a never-ending stream of Life, feeding the children of men, how long, how long shall it endure until man awakens and stands upon his feet?

This Great Mystery has the head of a lion, and in its eyes the light of daring and fortitude. The eyes are those of an human Soul looking out; searching the four quarters of the earth; looking, waiting, watching. Today the same as yesterday; the same puny creatures calling themselves men and women, with the same selfish traits, the same animal instincts to kill and rend and tear. And forever the same godlike forces struggling for birth within them! Yet the eternal patience waits.

O generations of pygmies! How long shall it be ere I trample ye with my lion's feet, and with my lion's mouth rend ye limb from limb? Eternal Justice demands your extinction, O bestial creatures who call yourselves kings of earth!

And yet, back of it all and crowning its head is the kingly Cap, the Ureus, the diadem of the King of Kings!

In those eyes so strong and fixed is the look of unutterable Love and Hope and Cheer. Looking always into the future, seeing innumerable suns rise and go down in blood-red fire, yet always waiting for the coming day.

O Love Divine! How long must ye wait? How many hearts must break with longing ere thy force conquers the evil in the world? This is thy message to the children of men:

Too long has the world groaned under perverted falsehoods calling themselves religions. Too long has priestcraft held mankind by the throat with lion's claws and lapped their blood.

Draw near to the Fount of Life.

Drink from the paps of Mother-love.

Draw great nourishing drafts of Life and be not discouraged.

Ye are not a stone image blindly crying out age after age the great story of man's redemption. Ye forget that ye are living, breathing vital forces with the power to act.

Ye too have stood on Egypt's sands and have given up your lives for the Great Cause; have been born again and again, struggled, hoped, despaired, and laid down your lives with trust in the Great Law. Yet always as life departed the vision of Reality is held before you.

There is an end to all things mundane; an end to long-continued waiting. I have waited through the ages and I crumble not, neither decay, because I symbolize to man this Eternal Waiting for the fullness of time, *ever looking toward the Light and knowing that it will come.*

Help mankind to see the Light.

Help them to shake off the shackles of superstition and priestcraft.

Help them to stand alone in the desert of human existence and look only toward the Rising Sun.

All things manifest in cycles, and it has been borne in on my stony heart that the Time is almost come; the great Cycle of Time has almost run its course.

There is a sacred scroll on which are the calculations of the incarnations which must be passed ere the deliverance comes. And since in ancient Egypt the first recognition of the Great Mystery was recorded in imperishable stone, so shall it there be fulfilled.

And She who came and went shall come again.

And the Spirit of Truth shall once more be taught.

The night is almost done and Egypt shall once more live in all her splendor and greatness as of yore. Not an earthly greatness, but a *spiritual illumination* through the *manifestation* of the eternal truths.

THE CURTAIN[2]

A Child of Light came down as a brooding Spirit, and was buried in the heart of the darkness. It parted the curtain of darkness with tiny hands of Flame. Then it became a glowing Eye. And the Eye smiled. And the Eye sent thrilling, life-giving forces through the darkness of the heart that was being born.

O little Flame, Within the dense darkness of my undeveloped heart! Help me to fix my gaze upon Thee. Help me to see the tiny flames which are thy hands pushing back the darkness of ignorance, glowing, brightening, illuminating, shining, shining behind the Curtain that hides the Other Side.

O little flaming Spirit of Light! As I sit and gaze the Curtain thins, opens, and I see thine Eye. And the Eye begins to smile at me through the Curtain. Love, Love, O Love Divine, where art Thou? What

---

[2] A vision seen by Harriette A. Curtiss, March 13, 1917. Transcribed and edited by F. Homer Curtiss, M.D., Secretary of the *Order of Christian Mystics*. Reprinted by permission from *Azoth Magazine*, July, 1917.

is this dark Curtain that hides thee from my gaze?

A still small Voice replies:

"The Curtain is the love of self. And into its meshes are woven the dark threads of personal opinion. Its warp and woof, woven in and out by the Loom of Time, are made up of so many, many threads."

Yet back of it I see the little Flame playing, lighting and illuminating. Must my tired fingers unravel thread by thread all this heavy Curtain? It has taken me so many weary ages to weave it. Look! Look! Into it I have woven so many beautiful pictures of the past; pictures of ambition, of desire for adulation, yea and many efforts to uplift humanity. Must these too be unravelled? See! If I rip out these threads my heart's blood will flow; for with them I see so cunningly devised all that I hold most dear. My intellect! What scintillating beams of light, like jewels, it has woven into the Curtain.

Beloved Child of the Flame, canst thou not look through the Curtain of my life and let thy beams illumine it into brightness? It is so great, so strong, so beautiful! And I love it! I love it! Come from behind its folds that I may see thee, bright shining Child. Be to it a beacon of Fire that the beauty of this my Curtain may shine forth more perfectly. Let thy Light make this my Curtain that I have woven through the ages more illumined and bright, that the world may see its beauty; for it hangs before the Holy of Holies. It drapes the Altar of the Most High.

O Holy Flame! Why dost thou flicker and die? Why dost thou cease thy brilliant shining? Come back! Come back! For without thy shining my Tapestry of Life fades into darkness. See its brilliant colorings! See its wondrous designs! O little Flame of Life! Shine upon it with thy brightness! Bless it with thy presence.

No! No! Thy Light grows dim. Thy brilliant Eye looks sad. Thy presence seems to recede deeper into the blackness of night. Ah me! I must watch and wait. I must pray before the Altar night and day. Then sometime thou wilt come back. Sometime thy bright shining will again appear.

O Flame of Love Divine! O Eye of Infinity! Once I caught a glimpse of thy bright shining, and now thou art gone! Why should this be? Where is my beautiful Tapestry? How can I see its glorious jewels and its wondrous colorings? How can the world discern it? It seems lost in the darkness of eternal night. Is this Divine Justice? that I should work and strive and weave and toil and hang before the Altar of the Most High this Tapestry of my life only to have the darkness hide it?

O Love Divine! One little spark of thy shining! One little thrill of thy coming! Without thy Light all I have done is lost. Without thy shining all is dark.

Methinks I slept and dreamed. And behold, in my dream I no longer saw the wondrous Curtain of my weaving. Instead I saw an Altar built of precious jewels. And beside it stood One all glory and brightness. And as I knelt before His feet I cried out with very ecstasy of joy. And then slowly my Curtain fell between us.

But what is this? What is this? Again the little Child of Light springs up. It is the Jewel of Fire whose tiny hands of Flame are reaching out. There is the glowing Eye that laughs in my face, yet it wears a countenance of plaintive joy.

And now I see it reach out its arms of Flame and touch the folds of my Tapestry. How beautifully it is illumined! The flames grasp it in their arms and hug it close. How they twist and shout and laugh for joy as they lick up and consume this my Curtain that I wrought so cunningly!

Let it burn! Let it burn! For it is the Flame of Love Divine that consumes it.

O Love Divine! O radiant Presence! Thou art still there. My curtain that I made, that I, even I, toiled and contrived and wove and builded is gone! The Flame of Love has consumed it. Only Thy Presence, now left undimmed and clear. Only that remains.

THE YOUNG AVIATOR RETURNS[3]

By Dr. & Mrs. F. Homer Curtiss

DURING our interview with the Young Aviator which was published in Azoth for September, 1918, he promised to play fair, and if he found we were correct in telling him that there was no death to the immortal Soul and that the change called death is but the taking off of a dense outer garment of flesh, he would return and admit that we were right. And he has kept his word.

Although that article was not presented as being evidential from the strictly scientific standpoint, but merely as an amusing and interesting incident, it was nevertheless severely criticized in a certain little sheet because it contained nothing but its own internal evidence as to being veridical. The criticism was unfair and bitter in its sarcasm and ridicule, especially in reference to the statement that the Young Aviator expected to study the models of the ancient Atlantean aeroplanes in the "Pattern Museum of the astral world" and endeavor through this study to help his country to win the supremacy of the air. Although this statement was ridiculed as the raving of unbalanced imagination on the part of the authors we had not deemed it worthy of reply, but on Sunday afternoon, January 5th, 1919, the Young Aviator again appeared to Mrs. Curtiss, this time in a highly indignant frame of mind. He insisted that he was the one whose veracity had been impugned and whose powers of ac-

---

[3] Reprinted by permission from *Azoth* for February, 1919.

curate observation had been slurred, hence he wished to vindicate the criticized statement. We therefore give herewith the substance of our talk with him, lasting from 5p.m. until nearly 6p.m., as reported by Mrs. Curtiss while in full waking consciousness according to the Independent or Telepathic method. It is not presented as scientifically evidential, but it was intensely interesting to us and we think it will be to most readers of Azoth. They are at perfect liberty not to take our word as to its source, if the message itself is not sufficient evidence, and we will not be offended if those who cannot respond to its truth lay it to our disordered imagination. We simply comply with the Young Aviator's request to transmit the message as he gave it to us.

"How do you do, Dr. Curtiss? I have been to see you a number of times, but you have always been in such a rush of work that I didn't like to butt in. I have also attended a number of your lectures and have also studied over here and have learned a lot since I first met you. My, but I was ignorant then! But I'm glad you have time to listen now because this is important. I especially want you to tell that Critic that all you said in that last article is true; for I have not only been admitted to that Pattern Museum and have studied the Atlantean aeroplane models, but I have come back and 'put across' what I have learned, although not in the way I then expected. And the U. S. Government is today building new types of aeroplanes embodying the new ideas I've been able to grasp and transmit. Already a plane has been announced that made 145 miles an hour on its trial flight, and another that carries sixty people. A Thanksgiving dinner was served to five people on another while 2,000 feet up. And soon you will hear of improvements far beyond anything known when I was down there, both as regards war-planes and especially planes which will make regular passenger travel as safe and commonplace as Pullman cars.

"You see, I've found out that when a man thinks definitely along a certain line there's a stream of force goes out from his brain that makes a pathway out into space. If he thinks clearly the path leads up through the realms and worlds—for I've found that there are many worlds over here beside the astral world in which I'm working—up to the ideal or pattern that his thought is reaching out toward. I've followed up lots of these paths since I've been over here just to see where they would lead, and although many of them start out bright and clear, nearly all just end in a jungle or are only blind alleys that get you nowhere. But the paths that go out from the minds of trained thinkers do lead to definite ends and bring back to those minds definite realizations or attainments. Once in a while I've found a mind like _____ whose path seems to go straight on upward, on and on through all the worlds as far as I can see and in each world it seems to spread out and make connections and make itself at home. Such a mind can bring back to its brain truth from every world it contacts, for I've followed it far enough to know that what you've said about life over here is true.

"My father's got a mind like that too. Oh, the path

that goes out from his brain is big and broad and clear and light. I certainly have a wonderful Dad! It's not occupied with philosophy and symbols and religious things like yours, but it's full of wonderful ways of helping humanity, of uplifting the people and improving conditions so they'll be better citizens. And he's got wonderful plans for our country, too; for making it the greatest and best and most helpful and wonderful country in the whole world. These paths are all bright and clear, but they only go a little ways, for back of each one there seems to stand a shrouded figure with a sickle in its hand and it cuts them off before they're finished. Poor Dad! I'm afraid he'll not last to see his great ideas fulfilled, for he's a broken man. He's like a great lion that's been put in a cage and beaten and prodded and half starved. His spirit is not broken, but his body is, so all he can do is to roar defiance. The fact is that Dad spends almost as much time over here with me now as he does with you down there, and every time I can get off from my work I go to him and tell him all about it.

"You said, Doctor, that more than a year ago your Teacher—O, yes, I've met your Teacher over here, but I don't get much time to study those things just now—told you that my Dad was going to sit with the Peace Council and have great influence in shaping its policies. When he wasn't appointed you thought perhaps you'd got things twisted or there had been some mistake. But you were told then that even though he wasn't officially appointed they couldn't keep him away, and it did look like it when he planned to visit the place where they

buried my body over in France. But I want to tell
you that your Teacher was right after all. He'll be
at the Peace Conference all right! But he may not
be there in just the way you thought! I can see that
he's not going to be with you long,[4] but I don't want
you to mention this as long as he is there, for that
thought in the minds of a lot of people would tend
to push him over here a little sooner. And when he
comes over here. . . .

"But I started out to tell that Critic how I 'put
across' the new ideas I get from my studies up here
in the Museum. In the first place everyone is not
admitted to it, any more than everyone is admitted
to the Masonic Library in Washington; only those
qualified. The Boche aviators over here want to get
in too, but as they never invented much of anything,
only copied others, and as they are still working
for 'Deutschland über Alles' they are not permitted
near the place. Also those who are merely curious
are barred. In fact there's just two classes who are
admitted, those of us over here who are interested
in making flying safer and more useful for mankind and those on earth whose thought-stream
makes a straight clear path right up to those patterns. And I'm told—although I don't know this
myself—that even so they would be prevented
from entering until the hour had struck when human evolution had reached a point where it would
be best for it to have such inventions, and many
more wonderful things are waiting for the years to

---

[4] EDITOR'S NOTE: This message was received about 5 P.M. on Sunday, the 5th of
January. Colonel Roosevelt died about twelve hours later.

come. Until then Those Who Have Charge up here keep the doors closed.

"Now there's a bunch of us boys up here who've given up our lives to the perfecting of flying, not merely given them up down there, but up here too; for we are devoting ourselves to it for the good of mankind. And having lost our lives in your world because of their deficiencies, we're going to find out how to make them safer. So when we learn something new about them we have to go to some of the inventors whose minds are sending out steady streams of thought toward flying. You see, I couldn't explain an improvement in the engine to Mrs. Curtiss. Even if I showed her every part and exactly how they worked she couldn't explain to a machinist how to make it. She hasn't that kind of mind; her pathways of light don't run toward the idea of flying.

"So we have to find those who are studying flying, and if they're sensitive enough we suggest the new improvement to them by impressing our idea upon them. And some of them get the idea more or less clearly, at least they make some changes in the old type. Of course they don't know they are being given the idea by us. They just think they 'thought it out' by themselves or they say 'It suddenly came to me,' etc., although some are conscious that they got help from somewhere in some way. With others we just put a picture or a model of the improvement in their thought pathway and let their thought-stream play all over it, and pretty soon they say, 'I see it! I've got the idea now.' And so they have. Some of them see it while over here in sleep and think they dreamed it all, but anyway we are getting the improvements 'over' as fast as the minds of the inventors can grasp them. Tell the Critic that I haven't been able to understand the engine that gets its power from the air yet, but I'm studying it, and when I get it I'll 'put that over' too.

"By the way, Doctor, I may not be telling you anything new, but I've found that there are places over here where they keep other kinds of ideas. There's one where they keep all the laws man has ever made and where all the plans of the great statesmen for the betterment of humanity and the improvement of its institutions and conditions are perfected and then stored up until some mind can reach up and grasp them, and the time is ripe to bring them down to earth. I don't know as you would call this a Museum, but it's some kind of a place like a State House or Forum or Academy or something like that. And only the great statesmen and rulers of the past can go in there, also the minds of the great statesmen on earth today which make straight paths into it.

"You know when my Dad comes over here he'll walk right in. Because he belongs there. My Dad certainly is a wonder! You know he used to be Julius Cæsar in a past life, but when he comes over here they're not going to call him that any more. They're going to call him. . . . as he's called on earth now, because they say over here that his present incarnation is a greater one than that as Cæsar, so they are going to call him. . . . Who was I in those days? Well, I'm ashamed to tell

you. Just call me my father's son.. . . . But since
Mrs. Curtiss has guessed it you can see that what I
did to him in that life, that I might rule in his stead,
has prevented me from succeeding him in this life,
and I thought I was doing the right thing then too.
It was 'not that I loved Cæsar less, but that I loved
Rome more.'

"And as he knows all the great statesmen on
earth today, when he gets over here, just as he
could hammer home fundamental truths and principles and 'put them over' on earth, so when he
gets here he will be able to hammer into the minds
of all the living statesmen, whose minds are all
open to his suggestions, the perfected ideas for the
good of mankind which he will find ready in this
Statesmen's Hall. So you see he may be a powerful
influence at the Peace Conference after all!

"Well, so long. I must run over and see how Dad
is getting along, but be sure to tell that Critic that
we are 'putting across' things of practical value to
mankind all the time. The trouble with him is that
he's not able to recognize them or understand where
they come from, because his mind-path doesn't run
in the right direction."

CHAPTER XXV

SOME FUNDAMENTALS IN THE PSYCHOL-
OGY OF NARCOTIC DRUG ADDICTION

by

DR. AND MRS. F. HOMER CURTISS
Founders of *The Order of Christian Mystics,* Authors of
"The Curtiss Books", etc., etc.

Read before the *World Conference on Narcotic Education*,
Philadelphia, Pennsylvania, July 6, 1926, by Dr. F. Homer
Curtiss, *Chairman* of the *Committee on Psychology*.

Mr. Chairman, and Ladies and Gentlemen of the Conference:
Yesterday this Conference was thrilled by the recital of the
many historic documents, organizations and movements which
have been inaugurated in Philadelphia, but to me, in addition to
all those things, there is a great, special, personal thrill in being
present at the inauguration of this Conference in this city; (applause) for it was in Philadelphia that The Order of Christian
Mystics, which we have the honor to represent, was founded.
And it was also here that I acquired my medical degree at the
University of Pennsylvania, my wife and my religion.

Mr. Chairman, if you and the Conference will pardon a personal reference. I would like to relate a personal reminiscence;
for it seems to me that this Conference stands in a similar position to that in which we stood many years ago, and the happy
result of the way our situation unfolded may be of encourage-
ment to the members of this Conference.

More than twenty years ago, Mrs. Curtiss and I were told to
prepare ourselves to launch a world-wide spiritual movement
presenting a cosmic philosophy which would give a ra-

tional explanation of all experiences in life, both here and hereafter.

At that time, this seemed impossible, hopeless. Naturally we thought that in the course of five or perhaps ten years of intensive study, we might possibly be ready to begin on a work of such magnitude, but when, after only one year's preparation, we were suddenly told: "It is time to begin the work," we were aghast. At that time, Mrs. Curtiss was employed as private secretary to the president of a large business concern; I was in my junior year in the medical school of the University of Pennsylvania, and instructor in the University and an active officer in a number of clubs and organisations, both within and outside the University. So I said: "How in the world can we begin the work? We have no time, no money, no prestige, no special ability, and we are unknown to the world. What can we do to start the work?" The answer was: "Get a pencil and a piece of paper." And that evening there was written the first announcement to the world of The Order of Christian Mystics and it is still in use today as the first page of the pamphlet explaining the work of the Order.

It seems to me, therefore, Mr. Chairman, and ladies and gentlemen, that this Conference today stands in a somewhat similar position. It has been given the vision. It has answered the call. It has come with its pencil and its piece of paper—its program—and I venture to predict that the document—its Constitution and Proceedings—which it will write at this time will be its guide and inspiration for many years to come.

For just as that half dozen earnest students gathered together in this city twenty years ago—conscious of the source of their inspiration, with faith in their mission, with the courage of their convictions, unselfish in their desire for the enlightenment of humanity, and strong in a childlike confidence in their ultimate success have seen their work grow from that first single sheet into thirteen large volumes of teachings all of which have run through many editions: and from a handful of students in this city until today there is not a civilized country on the face of the earth—including the native blacks in every country of West Africa from Morocco all the way down to Capetown—that is not represented, so may this Conference expect similar results; for it is following the same laws of growth.

Yesterday, our Secretary-General told us that this was the "King's Business," and let me assure you that those who are on the King's Business shall not fail to receive their credentials from Him. And if they look to Him as the source of their power and authority, they shall not fail to receive His help, His power, His inspiration and His love. (Applause.)

Let us then plant the seed-thoughts of our mission in the minds of all people, water them with our prayers, nourish them with our faith, and cultivate them with unselfish service, and I can assure you from personal experience, that the Lord of the Harvest will take care of the increase. And so I say to this Conference, no matter what the opposition and disappointments, follow your ideals and, "Sail on, sail on!" (Applause.)

Before beginning my paper, I wish to make a slight correction. From the program, it may seem that I prepared this paper all by myself, but such is not the case. Since this planet and its humanity have recently entered upon the great cycle of the new Aquarian or Woman's Age, it is especially fitting and a great pleasure for me to acknowledge the help, the collaboration and the inspiration of my wife, Harriette Augusta Curtiss, (applause) who with me, working as one, is the co-founder of The Order of Christian Mystics and the co-author of the entire series of "The Curtiss Books."

I now have the great privilege of presenting for your consideration, *Some Fundamentals in the Psychology of Drug Addiction*.

The mind of man is the instrument of his salvation; not the cause, only the instument. But his salvation depends upon the extent to which he understands the laws of mind and uses them wisely.

Back in the childhood days of modern psychology, before the development of psychical research, it used to be taught that thought was a secretion of the brain much as bile is a secretion of the liver. That was back in the days of purely materialistic and physiological psychology when we were taught that we think with our brains. As a result of modern research we now know, paradoxical as it may seem, that we do not think with our brains, but with our minds. Which is quite a different thing. For psychological research has proved that mind is the avenue through which the consciousness functions, and thus functions quite independent of the brain, the brain being but the mechanism which has to do with the expression on earth of the thought formulated in the consciousness.

This is an important advance over the now almost obsolete teaching of the old-school materialists in psychology that thought was impossible without the brain. But such a conception is only natural to those who are not familiar with the latest advances along this line so with your permission I would like to take a moment or two to refresh your minds as to certain recently ascertained fundamentals in this science, that I may the more easily point out their application to the problem of narcotic drug addiction.

No thought in the mind of man can find expression here except through muscular contraction. The use of the vocal apparatus, of the hand, the facial expression, a look, a shrug, all take place as a result of muscular contraction. In this respect the brain is but the switchboard by which an idea or current of thought, not in the brain but in the mind, contacts the body and stimulates those centers of muscular contraction which will give it proper expression in the physical world; pushes the button, as it were. The classical example in medical history of a laborer who, through a premature blast, had a crowbar driven up through the frontal lobes of his brain and survived without loss of his mental faculties, is an evidence of this. For although be lost many ounces of actual brain tissue the motor areas were not injured and so were able to function and express his thoughts.

For generations the mystery of how thought was translated into action, of how a thing so ethereal and intangible as thought could make contact with and find expression through so concrete and physical an instrument as the body, remained a mystery to medical science and the psychologists of the Western world, although it was well known for ages to the more profound psychologists and philosophers of the Far East. Modern researches have now confirmed and scientifically proved the Eastern teachings so that we now know that literally "thoughts are things," real, tangible, definitely formed objects composed of the substance of the mental world. In fact, they are so concrete that they can register themselves upon a photographic plate by their own inherent radiant energy, and quite independent of any form of light. Naturally it would be a misnomer to call the resulting pictures "thought photographs," as they are not photographs, since no form of photos or light was used. Therefore the term "skotograph" had to be coined to fit the case.

I, myself, have had the pleasure of seeing the original plate which included the first skotograph or thought-form. When Dr. Baraduc of Paris first conceived the idea he immediately experimented. He concentrated his gaze intently upon his walking-stick for several minutes until he could close his eyes and visualize it clearly. He then turned to his dark-room where he exposed an ordinary photographic plate in absolute darkness and gazed at it fixedly while concentrating his mind on the walking-stick and visualizing it intensely. When his concentration began to tire he stopped and developed the plate and there was a picture of the walking-stick clearly imprinted and surrounded by a slight halo of radiant energy.

After this experiment—which any one with strongly developed powers of concentration and visualization can duplicate un-

limitedly—hundreds of others were made, until it is now
scientifically well established that every thought we think
actually creates an objective—although invisible to the naked
eye—form, composed of mental molecules called "mentoids."
These thought-forms are clear or vague in outline according as
the concept held in the mind is clear or vague; they are strong
and positive or dim and weak according to the strength of the
desire or the character of the thought that creates them. They
have forms characteristic of the idea which fashions them, and
even impregnate the photographic film with their characteristic
color, the colors varying with the state of the emotions, the
health, etc. And I have seen those colors, not placed on the
film, but embedded within its substance. They also have their
rates of vibration and even sound their keynote, although it is
not audible to the ordinary ear.

These thought-forms are charged with a form of radiant
energy according to the thought-force and will-power used in
their production. All this has been demonstrated, not only in the
thousands of experiments of Dr. Baraduc and his followers, but
also in quite another field, that of Psychic Research. So powerfully radio-active are these thought-forms that their formative
activity can affect not only the photographic plate or film, but
also that newly discovered semi-physical, semi-astral, biologic
plasma called ectoplasm, which certain relatively rare individuals endowed with a special development of their etheric and
astral bodies are capable of extruding from their physical bodies.

This ectoplasm first emanates as a vapory cloud, but after
slight contact with the air condenses into a semi-solid, cold,
clammy, jelly-like mass which has been weighed, measured,
photographed before a moving-picture camera, and submit-
ted to biological and microscopical analyses, etc. All this is
familiar to advanced students of psychic research, but the
point to be noted in this connection is that the creative power
of thought and the radio-active emanations of thought-forms
can mold or impress upon the plastic ectoplasm any form or

thought held strongly in the minds of those present. This has been amply demonstrated in hundreds of experiments in private psychological laboratories under the most exacting and rigidly scientific test conditions, many actual photographs of which can be seen in Dr. von Schrenck Notzing's "Phenomena of Materialization," also in "From the Unconscious to the Conscious," by Dr. Gustave Geley, the late director of the Institute Metapsychic of Paris, in Sir Arthur Conan Doyle's "The Case for Spirit Photography," in Dr. Coates' "Photographing the Invisible,"[1] etc., etc. These thought-forms can also act upon solutions of certain specially prepared mineral salts so as to cause the form to crystallize out of the solution in a solid mass of mineral deposits, as described by Dr. Charles W. Littlefleld in his book "The Beginning and Way of Life."

For countless ages it has been a common thing for mankind to use such expressions as "currents of thought," "prevailing ideas," "trains of thought," "an idea suddenly struck me," etc., etc. Now we see not only the truth of these expressions, but their rationale and scientific explanation. For these thought-forms, once created and launched into the atmosphere of the mental world, naturally tend—through a law analogous to the law of chemical affinity, the Law of Mental Affinity—to gather together with other thought-forms of like character and vibratory rate. These aggregations of mass thought are capable of exercising terrific dynamic power varying with their constitution, as is seen in their generally destructive effect in the so-called "mob psychology" and "crowd hysteria," which is capable of sweeping people into ferocious expressions of prejudice, hatred and passion, without regard to law or reason, and quite opposed to the normal thoughts and desires of the same individuals when not under the obsession of such thought aggregates.

The constructive side of the same law of mass-thought is

[1] See also *Psychic Science*, London, January, 1925, April, 1925, January 1926.

seen not only in religious services and mass-prayer action, in which spiritual forces are invoked to vitalize and make more powerful the thought-forces, but is also seen in aroused public opinion so-called, but which is simply the aggregation of similar thought-forms directed toward a definite end. Its compelling action is so great that it can quickly settle a coal strike or even the recent great "general strike" in England, the constructive thought-forms generated for the common good neutralizing and finally overpowering the personal and selfish thought-forms of individuals or smaller groups.

The gradual aggregation of the thought-forms of both temperance and woman's suffrage, generated at first by a handful of altruistic and far-seeing Souls, but persistently repeated and endowed with positive will and great spiritual power, at last swept the whole nation and finally amended the Constitution of the United States! During the World War, after "The Order of Christian Mystics" had inaugurated a world-wide noon-day prayer service for peace among its pupils throughout the world, the idea was taken up by many churches and other organizations, and within a few weeks the lust for war and the will to fight of the Central Powers was neutralized and overcome by the Will for Peace thus consciously generated. The Central Powers then made overtures for an armistice, not because they could not have fought on for months so far as guns, ammunition and supplies were concerned, but because of a so-called "loss of morale," both in the ranks and at home. *This was a purely psychological reaction* which produced the concrete result which saved millions of human lives and reshaped history and human destiny.

Even so must we apply this same law of mass-thought action to this terribly menacing problem of drug addiction. The so-called campaign of education which this Conference is organized to promote is nothing less than a plea consciously to generate en masse at least two generic thought-forms; one *the danger of the use* of narcotic drugs, the other the *abolition of the possibility of obtaining them.* (Applause.) But if we have an understanding of this basic law of mass-thought creation and projection we can work more consciously, intelligently and efficiently toward its consummation and generate thought-forms and thought currents with such power in the aggregate that they shall *sweep the country and demand and command* their expression and enforcement. (Applause.) Indeed, it is not outside the bounds of possibility to *procure a Constitutional amendment* in this country and the adoption of *universal abolition of narcotic drugs* by all the peoples of mankind! (Applause.)

Another point of importance in this connection. The mind of man is enormously open to suggestion. We may lay it down as a fundamental law of psychology that every thought we think or accept as ours sooner or later *tends to express itself* in action *through us, unless counteracted* by an opposite thought of greater power. Many, many thoughts and suggestions pop into our minds that are not ours at all. Created by others and floating along the thought-currents of the community, they drift into our minds when they are in a relaxed or idle state—the doors of our mind swinging idly on their hinges, as it were—or because of affinity or similarity of vibration to our own. But if we accept these outside thoughts, take them in and contemplate them, we have deliberately made them our own and given them power over us. For another fundamental law of psychology is that every thought that we contemplate or repeat we feed and give power over us.

Therefore, a feature of the educational work which this Conference is to inaugurate should be to teach the people of the world—especially its youth—the laws of suggestion; that they must be on their guard against all suggestions and accept none without conscious scrutiny to see if it is in harmony with their ideals and standards of life before consciously adopting it and making it their own. For we are mentally and morally, and even legally responsible, not only for our acts and words, but for every thought to which we give expression. They must be taught to recognize that any sug-

gestion which tends to influence them to violate the law, the
moral code and their ideals and standards of life is vicious and
should be *immediately counteracted* by the strongest possible
assertion of *the opposite thought*. They will thus recognize that
the suggestion of the drug peddler that they take a sniff or a
"shot" to "get a thrill" or to "be a sport" or to "try anything
once" is not a casual and friendly suggestion or even a harmless
dare, but is a coldly calculated and deliberate stab in the back, a
deliberate attempt to break down their natural psychic immunity
solely for the sordid money there is in it. Far better "take a dare"
than embrace a devil.

   The above is the general application of psychological laws to
this problem. But there are many personal applications of which
I will outline but one. But just as the specialist in science, when
baffled by problems in the known range of his specialty, must
preserve an open mind and be willing to go outside the orthodox
limits and go into unknown fields if necessary, grapple with
entirely new conceptions and be ready to accept truth wherever
found, if his science is to advance and not get into a rut, so must
we in the consideration of this problem of narcotic drug addiction. I therefore trust that you will bear with me in patience for
a few minutes while I enter upon a subject outside the narrowly
materialistic lines to which this problem is usually confined, a
subject which is such a wide-spreading and to many, obscure
and tabued specialty that reference to it may arouse a certain
amount of incredulity, or even opposition, in the minds of those
who have not given the subject special thought or whose minds
may be prejudiced by early training in a materialistic conception of life or by the remnants of certain medieval superstitions.

   After proving the concrete and objective reality of thought-
forms—even though as invisible as a gas or an electron the
next step was the proof that these thought-forms could be
projected to and registered upon the mind properly attuned
to the mind of the sender, and without regard to distance.
This direct transfer of thought from mind to mind without

any means of physical expression or communication is called telepathy. The proof of this power has been abundantly set forth in the classical volume of F. W. H. Myers, "The Human Personality", in "Phantasms of the Living" by Gurney, Myers and Podmore, and by many later investigators, some of whom have had as high as 78 per cent accurate results.

The next step after proving possible the direct and independent communication of mind with mind was to reveal that this law operated no matter what the environment of the mind; that is, whether the mind was embodied or disembodied. Beside the classical works referred to above there are many later volumes packed with such a mass of evidence in proof of this that it is now scarcely open to discussion in well informed circles.

My new point, therefore, is that just as the mind of those embodied here on earth can create and project thought-forms, and also receive them, so can the disembodied mind of the excarnate create and project and receive thought-forms. This they can do far more easily and with greater power than the incarnate because not hampered by the inertia of a physical instrument of expression, the body of flesh; also by the inertia of the mass-thought of humanity on any subject, as well as the tendency of the rational mind to argue it out before being able to accept a new idea.

Modern research has abundantly and scientifically proved— through photography, telekinesis, cross-correspondence, book-tests, etc., etc.—that so-called death applies to the physical instrument or body only and *not to the mind or the personality*, the essential individual or Soul. So-called death is but a slipping off of an outer garment, a coat of flesh, the personality—thereby being released from its hampering conditions and limitations and becoming, not a bright and shining, all-perfect angel, but remaining almost exactly as it was before, except that it is not hampered by the physical instrument so necessary to relate its consciousness to the physical world.

That the mind and consciousness does thus survive and is

capable of giving viridical proof of its identity and continued existence is proved by its ability to mold the exudations of ectoplasm into a simulacrum of its former physical body so perfect as to be easily recognized by its surviving friends and in some cases which I have seen so complete that it can be temporarily inhabited by the discarnate personality and be used to walk, talk audibly in its characteristic tone of voice, move physical objects and otherwise manifest and conclusively prove its identity and its relatively unchanged mental and other personal idiosyncrasies.

This being the case—and the volumes of evidence made under scientific test conditions place the subject almost out of the realm of controversy except as to details, it now being simply a question of the amount of information or lack of information one has on the subject—the person who departs from this physical world with any strong earthly or bodily desire unsatisfied naturally seeks every possible avenue through which to gratify that desire. And if it is a desire which can be gratified only in the physical world it naturally seeks an instrument or physical body through which it can obtain such gratification. This desire for renewed physical expression holds such minds close to the physical world in what may be called the slums of the ethereal or astral world, which is the world just beyond and an octave higher in vibration than the physical world. The discarnate personalities thus held close to earth by their desires and thoughts constitute what are called the "earth-bound," while those not so held by earthly desires naturally and unconsciously rise into the higher, finer and brighter realms of manifestation according to the Law of Spiritual Gravity.

To obtain the desired expression in the physical the disembodied one must find some person whose body and mind are abnormally open to such suggestions, impressions and thought-transference to the point of at least partial possession or obsession. Such persons are found among the mentally unstable, the neurasthenic, and especially among the alcoholics and narcotic drug addicts. I use the words "abnormally open to such impressions" advisedly, for the very good reason that just as the majority of humanity are protected from the invasion of infectious diseases by a natural physical immunity—until that immunity is broken down by fatigue, destructive emotions, abnormal living, etc.—just so is the mind of man protected from the invasion of psychic suggestions and thought-forms from the invisible worlds by a natural psychic immunity. Therefore, let no normal mind fear psychic invasion.

We all possess an ethereal and astral body as the substratum or model into the meshes of which the physical body is built. And between this finer body and the physical body there is a special layer of etheric matter which normally prevents vibrations and thought-forces from the unseen world from reaching and registering upon the physical body. But this protective and immunity-conferring layer is dissolved by alcohol and is paralyzed and rapidly disintegrated by narcotic drugs, thus exposing the addict to obsession from the invisible just as one whose physical immunity is destroyed is open to infection by invisible pathogenic bacteria. The alcohol radical of all the higher alcohols—methyl, ethyl, propyl, butyl, etc.—is really an ethereal substance normally belonging in the ethereal world but temporarily materialized in the physical. When its bonds to the physical are released it naturally tends to fly back to the world and octave of vibration to which it normally belongs. In the alcoholic it passes into the ethereal world through certain outlets or centers which connect the physical with the astral, and in doing so it dissolves the etheric wall which normally confers psychic immunity, and thus exposes the victim to all the horrors to be found in the slums of the astral world. The horrid visions of delirium tremens are therefore not the mere ravings of a disordered imagination, but actual sights of very real things in the astral world.[2]

The narcotic radical in drugs acts in a similar manner, ex-

---

[2] For a full explanation of all after-death conditions see *Realms of the Living Dead*, Curtiss.

posing its victim not only to his own *physical* craving for the drug, but also to the much greater and more sinister force of obsession by disembodied addicts who seek such abnormally opened channels for the gratification of their still persisting desire. This accounts for the powerful and all-compelling or so-called "irresistible impulse" which overwhelms the weakened wills of even those who are seemingly cured by proper institutional treatment the moment they are released into the outer world, where the drug can be obtained.

But even these earth-bound discarnate addicts can be educated to cease their obsessing influence as is illustrated by a message recently received by Dr. Wickland[3] of Los Angeles, Cal., from Wallace Reid, the well-known motion-picture star, who committed suicide in despair of ever curing his drug addiction. Dr. Wickland reports him as saying: "I was in such misery and so helpless that many spirits demonstrated through me, and I had no one who understood how to help me conquer the soul craving. . . . Many, many, come back and try to get the drug, even a little bit. . . . and they ruin others against their will. I knew many times that I myself did not want it, but there was such a strong power back of me! If the world could only know! . . . Oh, if I could only warn and help others!—Why did not some one warn me?" We understand that many such cases have been cured in Dr. Wickland's clinic. It is just such a warning that this Conference is organized to give, so no such a reproach to our civilization can again be made. (Applause.)

This fact of psychic obsession also accounts for those crimes of "irresistible impulse" of which the perpetrator knows nothing after the obsessing influences pass away and he returns to his normal consciousness. All such belong to the same class as the drug addict, namely, the self-indulgent, weak-willed or hyper-sensitive individuals who allow the doors of their minds to swing idly to and fro in negative mental states, or those whose psychic immunity has been weakened or destroyed, both

[3] *Thirty Years Among the Dead*, Wickland, 168-170

of which make them easy victims to the inrush of any outside but positive and determined thought-force. There is a vast difference however, not only in degree *but in kind*, between strong telepathic suggestions from the mental and spiritual worlds and a definite psychic invasion from the astral world; all the difference between an unlifting spiritual inspiration and a demonical possession.

It should be remembered that sudden and strong impulses from the invisible—both good and evil, constructive and destructive, inspiring and depressing—come not in words—unless one is clairaudient—but by the inrush of a new idea or current of thought-force, which makes a compelling and often overwhelming impression. Those of positive mentality, developed wills and high moral character are able to check and control such inrushes until they can examine them and decide what their reaction should be. But those of weak mentality or will, who are hyper-sensitive to outside impressions, tend to give way to and express such impulses without due consideration. They respond to the negative or evil suggestions more readily because such usually appeal to some form of self-indulgence, or because they require less exertion of positive will than the good and constructive impulses. Hence, mental poise and acute discrimination is a vital point to be taught in any campaign of education on any subject.

During the World War thousands were induced to use narcotic drugs, not only to ease their discomforts and suffering and to forget the horrors of war, but also to give them the reckless pseudo fighting-courage of the addict and enable them to play the grandiose part which is one of the symptoms of drug addiction. And the sudden passing over into the invisible world of thousands of such addicts, in the full tide of life and still ruled by strong earthly desires has been an important psychic factor in the alarming increase of narcotic drug addiction since the war. Yesterday, we were told by one of the speakers, that since the confirmed drug addict cannot be cured, the only solution to the problem was to "kill them off." From what we have said above you will see that, apart from all humanitarian considerations, such a course would be the worst thing that could be followed; in fact, this is the fundamental psychological argument against all capital punishment. For as long as those who are dangerous to society are kept confined, society is protected from them; but if we destroy their physical bodies, we simply send them out into the astral world where they can prey upon humanity, ten, a hundred, yes, a thousand times more viciously than if they were set free while still in the flesh.

From the above hasty survey we see that narcotic drug addiction is far more than a habit. It is a definite psychic disease, affecting the etheric and astral bodies primarily and the physical body only secondarily. This is evidenced by the fact that, just as no destructive or structural changes can be found in the brains of those suffering from certain psychic types of insanity, neither can they be found in the tissues of the drug addict, even by our best pathologists. The fact that the chemical end-products of narcotic drugs are practically unknown, and our physiological chemists can find no trace of the drug in the excreta, is not at all surprising, because it has simply passed through the physical body into the astral world, whence its essence originated, leaving perhaps only a trace of its irritating passage in a slight inflammation of the liver and gall-bladder.

Other drugs which produce sleep also open the door into the invisible world and permit the consciousness to leave the body, but with less corroding and degenerating effects upon its psychic unity.

As a matter of fact nearly all the alkaloids and vital essences, as well as flavors, perfumes, etc., in all vegetation, are really ethereal substances from the invisible worlds materialized in the physical through the synthesizing power of the life-force of the plant and so temporarily manifesting on earth. All that really belongs to the physical world is the little that is left behind as ash when the plant is burned. All else comes from the invisible and returns again to its source.

The common fear of mankind of having anything to do with the disembodied is an instinct which has been a boon to the unenlightened masses of mankind in general, for it has acted as a factor in protecting its psychic immunity and has thus served an excellent purpose in the preservation of the race. But fear is dispersed by knowledge. And in these enlightened days, while fear still has its value for the vast mass of the unenlightened and less advanced, it must be overcome by the proper education of those who are ready to enter into new fields of consciousness. But there is still great danger unless this is done with a full knowledge of at least the basic laws of the realm to be invaded. Hence the promiscuous dabbling in psychic matters as a pastime or as a means of amusement and without proper instruction in its laws and danger, is as dangerous as to let a group of children play unattended in the generator room of a giant electric plant.

Drug addiction can, therefore, be treated with a hope of permanent cure only by a recognition of its underlying psychic as well as physical factors. For even after apparent physical cure the victim is never safe until he is thoroughly drilled in watching for and recognizing the suggestions, both of his old associates, his environment, the drug peddlers and the "irresistible impulse" of the disembodied, and, furthermore, has had his will developed and strengthened to the point where he can neutralize and overcome such suggestions in his own strength, or with the help of those higher powers and spiritual forces which are invoked through prayer and aspiration, and he should remain under control until he has proved such ability. This is the most important point in completing the permanent cure of the addict, for it is doubtful if the etheric wall between the two worlds can be regenerated and rebuilt with sufficient stability to give unconscious psychic immunity.

Let me now pause to emphasise the statements made yesterday by Major Brewster and confirmed to me personally by Dr. O'Connor. You will remember that these gentlemen are in charge of the Narcotic Section of the New York City

Department of Correction, Major Brewster being the Warden
and Dr. O'Connor the Medical Expert of that institution.
Since they are the heads of this department in the largest city
in the world, they are probably the greatest living authorities
on their aspect of this problem. And when they tell us, after
an experience with twenty to thirty thousand patients coming
under their treatment: when they tell us, as Major Brewster did
yesterday, that as far as they know, out of that great mass or
army only a few—I think he said five or six that he knew of,
after the physical results had been cured and they had gained
thirty to forty pounds in weight, become robust in physical
health—*only five or six could survive temptation and relapse*
after they went back to the outer world where the drugs could
be obtained. And why? These few, Major Brewster said, were
among those who had only a slight addiction, whose cases were
not chronic and who had not gone on to the enormous doses of
the chronic users.

Now, what is the meaning back of such a statement as his, its
significance? I hold that it absolutely confirms the contention
of my thesis, because these were cases which had not gone to
the point where the power of will in the patient had become
absolutely destroyed, so they were able, through the exercise
of their will, decidedly to resist the inrush of the suggestions
and temptations that come to the addict when he returns to his
old environment. In other words, their psychic immunity had
not been completely destroyed.

You will notice, if you study the program of this Conference,
a remarkable thing: that the medical profession tell us that
there is no cure for the confirmed drug addict, and there is
not one proposition presented on the whole program of this
Conference of a curative or constructive nature for the help
of the addict. There is one paper on a later day presenting a
remedy for the spread of the addiction perhaps, but not one
for the cure of the addict. But in this paper I hope I have
presented to you a constructive, practical, rational and psychologically sound method of completing the cure and of

bridging that all-important gap between the *physical cure* and the *psychic cure*; and that is by the proper instruction and control of the physically regenerated person as to his psychological responsibility and his ability to resist psychic invasion and suggestion.

All drug cases, therefore, in my opinion, should be kept confined apart from society until they have been so trained and have so demonstrated their ability to maintain their psychic immunity and self-control under tempting conditions that they will not respond to the appeals made to them under such terrible circumstances.

Dr. Hubbard: How long will that take?

Dr. Curtiss: It depends on the case and the amount of treatment.

Now, therefore, I take the liberty of presenting—and I hope that some delegate of this Conference will feel impelled to present this as a resolution—certain recommendations which I feel are not fanatical, but are sane and psychologically sound and non-controversial in character. I therefore recommend that, in addition to whatever other means this Conference adopts in its educational program, it will include the necessary specific teaching as to these definite psychological principles:

First: the power of suggestion and *the means of neutralizing* adverse suggestions:

Second: the personal responsibility of every one, not only for his acts and words, *but also for his thoughts*:

Third: the necessity for conscious discrimination before accepting *any* suggestion or *any* thought and reacting to it, and

Lastly: the necessity for cultivating self-reliance and independence.

In closing, permit me to quote two stanzas of a well-known hymn:

"Down from their home on high,
Down through the starry sky,
Angels, descending, fly,
While the earth shaketh;

Roll they the stone away,
From where the Savior lay.
Out into glorious day
His way He taketh."

Let us pray that this Conference shall so invoke the uplifting and inspiring angelic forces of light, life and power from the spiritual realms that they shall descend "down through the starry sky" of our unselfish thought for the salvation of mankind, while those earth-bound souls who traffic in the youth of the world shall tremble. (Applause.)

Understanding scientifically and precisely what we are doing, may the organized and psychologically planned world-wide campaign of narcotic education inaugurated by this Conference roll away the stone of ignorance and prejudice which has so long imprisoned the higher, spiritual or Christ-consciousness, the Savior of mankind that it may come forth from the tomb of materialism, as, free and unhampered, out into the glorious day of spiritual realization of the essential brotherhood and oneness of all mankind, "His way He taketh." Amen. (Applause.)

Chairman Hobson: This is a very remarkable paper to which we have listened. It is now open for discussion, but before the discussion begins may I ask the Doctor one question? In Los Angeles a perpetual revival goes on; I have found cured addicts at that revival who would go down amongst their fellow addicts in the same environment and remain cured—I don't know for how long. Have you any explanation for that? Having been cured in the revival and remaining cured after that?

Dr. Curtiss: I think a little serious consideration of my paper will give the answer. Such cases are the result of something that the medical profession cannot duplicate. The result is brought about, as I said, first through definite currents of spiritual force and second by definite spiritual helpers who are positively invoked. They have been known to help build up the weakened will and to establish self-control. During that time they have helped to protect the unfortunate addict from obsessing entities because he is conscious of that presence with him which will bring about his freedom from this slavery.

Dr. Hubbard: So divorced, or at least not necessarily connected, are these four points that the speaker has presented, so not connected with any mystic philosophy, that *I am sure we can all agree to these four points.* I am certain that we have no differences in regard to them. But there is a question about our joining forces with another kind of philosophy. Is it not true that the unnaturally depraved appetite within and the sinister temptations of the dope peddler are consorted to break down the man's resistance against that form of evil without invoking the power of disembodied spirits? . . . I believe and feel certain that the unnatural, depraved appetite within gives an easy response to the temptation of the dope peddler, and I am sure we get the result without unnecessarily involving ourselves in a philosophy which we have never entertained. I do not think that we are called upon to take up a new philosophy in order to deal practically with this problem. I am satisfied to take the speaker's word that if we think strongly, persistently, sensibly along the right line of activity for a proper aim we can have it. And by thinking strongly and consistently, perpetually, of a noble resolve, a high ideal, such as an amendment to the Constitution, we can have it. . . .

Dr. Curtiss: I call the attention of the Conference to the fact that I have not asked the Conference to subscribe to any new psychic philosophy at all, but simply to more firmly establish certain fundamental psychological educational principles. I merely used the psychic philosophy to give you a rational and scientific understanding of what takes place, both physically and psychically, in drug addiction and what is necessary to perfect a cure. Now, as to the naturally depraved tendencies of mortal man producing addicts, it cannot be.

Even the naturally depraved mortal must actually take the narcotic and that is what breaks down the natural psychic immunity of the subject And so he proceeds with his self-indulgence: he proceeds with his woeful violation of spiritual Jaw, and there is a consequent destruction of all will power and a realization of his utter failure to cope with any situation that he is brought face to face with.

Dr. Ward: As I listened to Dr. Curtis? remarkable paper, two thoughts occurred to me: One was a point that he called attention to and that is that his is the only paper on the Agenda that deals with the psychological aspects of the subject, and that means the inner responsibilities. These four points which Dr. Curtiss brought forth, and Dr. Curtiss' investigations and paper, to me indicate a direct answer to a rampant modern philosophy, the philosophy of modern criminology. . . . which holds that man is not a responsible being; that to talk of his psychology from the sense of the Spirit is useless and a waste of time. Dr. Curtiss' paper is a direct answer to that The regeneration of man can come only from his inmost Soul, and to treat man simply as a sort of machine, without responsibility without any obligation to his God, is aimed at the destruction of society. We can only view man as a responsible agent in possession of a will which he must answer for one day to his God, and I think Dr. Curtis? Paper heartily supports that thesis. . . . He did stress one point, that there was only one cure and that was that self-discipline is the salvation of the drug addict And he said that the responsibility for drug addiction, the ultimate responsibility, lies with our educators who do not recognize a definite authoritative morality, and on the other band, with the parents of the children who are not responsible for every moment of their time. . . . The child from its earliest years must be taught that it is a moral agent and responsible for its life, responsible for its Soul to God. . . .

A resolution embracing the four recommendations made by Dr. Curtiss was passed by a unanimous vote and referred to the Committee on Resolutions.

INDEX

Achilles, 34
Adepts, 237
Aeroplanes, 106, 260, 291-2-6
Age, Aquarian, 268; in astral, 91
Alcohol, effect of, 116, 125
Ambition, stimulated, 140
Angels, 248, 278
Anger, 141
Annunciation, the, 260
Arnold, Sir Edwin, quoted, 43, 67, 87
Asleep, when, 47
Astral, activities in, 48, 51; advice, 215;
    age in, 91; animals in, 45, 57; avoid
    cannot, 38; beauty of, 141; body dies, 83,
    184; body intermediary, 58; body, looks
    of, 59, 92; body of mediums, 59; body
    modified, 106; body, radiance of, 46;
    born into, 29, 67; chill, 229; classified,
    12; clothing, 77, 95-7, 257; colors, 104;
    conflicting reports, 41; currents, 60, 104;
    day and night in, 44; double, 57; eating,
    51-3, 257; entities, 54-6, 70-1-9, 109,
    129, 134-6, 149, 150-9, 215-17, 230;
    faced, 21; glamor, 130-3, 228; includes,
    22-3; interpenetrates, 23; journeys in,
    51-3; life in, 47; light in, 146; lusts,
    129; location of, 24; material is, 23, 39;
    meaning of, 15; not subconscious, 12;
    objects in, 45, 76; odors, 104; protection
    in, 56, 79, 127; radiance of, 46; reality
    of, 21; Realms of, 37, 40-1; Red Cross
    in, 48; scenery, 43; schools, 88, 187;
    sheaths, 116; shells, 54-5; sleep in, 60-1;
    things reversed, 44; time in, 93-4; water
    in body, 51; weapons cut, 76, winds, 61
Atma, 243
Avatar, 240, 271
Avesha, 205
Aviators, Great Adventure, 253; Returns,
    291
Awakening, 62-7

Baptism, for the dead, 49
Birth, gate of, 42; into astral, 29, 67-8

Black, Brotherhood, 190; wearing, 65-6
Blavatsky, Mme., 44; still working, 194
Blood, astral lavender, 76; attracts
    elementals, 79; in operations, 79
Body, astral, 46, 51-8, 83, 106; psychic,
    184; spiritual, 239

Cabinet, materializing, 102
Caduceus, 249
Caesar, Julius, 297
Challenge, everything, 227; the Christ, 127,
    142, 226
Charon, 30
Charybdis, 33
Chill, astral, 229
Christhood, 236
Clairaudience, 202
Clairsentience, 202
Clairvoyance, 201
Clothing, astral, 77-8, 95-7, 257
Colors, 104, 196
Communication, by telegraph instrument,
    24; described, 197; examples of
    independent, 253; independent used,
    13; justified, 198; methods of, 200;
    subjective methods, 213; telepathic
    method, 225: unquestionable, 25
Cord, umbilical, 28
Creations, thought, 70-2-5-7, 99, 133; must
    redeem, 147
Cremation, 65
Cross, Red, 48
Curtain, The, 287

Dances, 248
Dangers, real, 13, 22, 32-7, 70, 199
Darkness, outer, 103, 146, 276
Death, a withdrawal, 58; Angel of, 34;
    condition after, 215; fighting after,
    69; gate of, 42; in disasters, 48, 69;
    on battlefields, 68-9; realize no, 63-4;
    sudden, 68

www.ingramcontent.com/pod-product-compliance
Lightning Source LLC
Chambersburg PA
CBHW051814090426
42736CB00011B/1473